Market Mojo

The Beginner's Guide to the Stock Market

Kathy G. Mills

Printed in the United States of America
First Printing, 2017

For Leath and Ava

Contents

Introduction

Welcome to *Market Mojo*, the book that will inspire you to take your financial future into your own hands. This informative text provides a foundation for your stock market knowledge—from learning key terms and concepts all the way to understanding intimidating acronyms and advanced computations. If you are one of the millions of Americans who shy away from investing because you think you lack the proper knowledge to do so, then this book is for you.

In an effort to make the underlying philosophy of *Market Mojo* clear, here are a few things you should know before we begin:

- I do not promise to make you rich. (Though I sincerely wish you the best with that endeavor.)
- I do not give "hot tips" or claim "insider knowledge" of the stock market that will give you an edge over other investors. (Frankly, you should be leery of books that *do* make those claims.)
- I do not tell you how to invest your money.

There are plenty of other financial books on the market with that kind of focus. You are welcome to go that way if you wish, but I'd like to take you down a different path. My sole purpose in writing this book is helping readers understand the *foundations* of investing. After all, we don't walk before we crawl, and we don't start spelling words before we've learned the alphabet. Why then, would we attempt to invest our money before we really know how the market works? Like any other important skill, investing knowledge is best acquired by taking deliberate and progressive steps. To that end, this book will do the following:

- Provide an overview of how stock markets work;
- Offer step-by-step descriptions and demonstrations when calculations are used; and
- Discuss the pros and cons of different approaches to investing.

In short, I've devised a way for you to quickly pick up the financial education that you probably didn't get in school. I've done the research, I've organized the topics, and I've laid everything out in a logical format. In this age of information overload, a clear and straightforward manual is the perfect solution for cutting through the noise and getting down to the basics.

"Market Mojo" is more than just a snappy title; it's a quality that is quite real and extremely valuable to a potential investor. A precise definition of "mojo" is hard to pin down, but it generally suggests a special ability that allows its users to act with conviction and confidence. Furthermore, mojo is unique. While many people may have it, no two people will exhibit it in the same way. When you use mojo, you know what your goal is, you know what to do to achieve that goal, and you expect nothing less than complete success. Mojo empowers you to take active steps to realize your vision for the future, which is why you should apply these principles to your finances as well. With a little focused study, you should be able to evaluate different investing options, weigh their merits, and create an individualized investing plan that reflects *your* needs and *your* goals. That is what Market Mojo is all about.

Although learning about investing is a process, it doesn't have to be a long, boring, or complicated one. Forget about the stodgy textbooks and the overly complex articles you've read while trying to get a handle on the stock market. This book will build your knowledge incrementally by presenting engaging lessons, comprehensive vocabulary lists, and periodic quizzes in an informal narrative style that make the topic approachable and fun. That's right. I said *fun.*

Getting your mojo has never been this easy. Just turn the page to get yours up and running now.

Part 1

To Market, To Market!

The Parable Principle
Ain't Nothin' Free, Baby
The SEC Is the Boss of Me
(Ex) Ch-ch-ch-ch-ch-ch-CHANGES!
Hi-Ho, Hi-Ho, to IPO We Go . . .

To Market, To Market!

This section of the book will use a fictional business as a case study to explain some important fundamental concepts. It will answer the following questions:

- Why does a company issue stock?
- What process does a company go through to offer shares of its stock for sale?
- What risks do companies take when selling stock?
- How does buying stock benefit investors?
- What risks do investors take when buying stocks?

If you decide to invest without really knowing how the Wall Street machine works, you're essentially tossing your hard-earned money into a wishing well and hoping for the best. That's why your stock market education will begin by cracking the machine open and taking a look at the individual parts. If you understand how investing works from the inside out, you are in a much better position to make sound judgments and informed decisions when it *is* time to invest.

Let's Get This Party Started!

I'm a big fan of using storytelling as a teaching method. There isn't a single concept out there that can't be easily explained with a lively and entertaining story. And since my goal is to demonstrate that learning about the stock market doesn't have to be the dull, dry experience that it's often made out to be, I have packed this jaunty little tome with amusing anecdotes, saucy spiels, and yes, even a few poignant parables. (Honestly, I should ask my editor if this book should be reclassified as a thriller.)

The first story is about my very own business, Kathy's Accordion Café.

(Fig. 1.1)

I've always been passionate about accordions and coffee, so starting this café was a natural extension of my interests and abilities. It's a very chic establishment modeled after the Café Imperial in Prague. Patrons gather here for coffee and pastries while enjoying their favorite soft-rock 70s hits performed by classically trained accordionists. (Stop smirking. My café = my rules, OK?)

It pretty much looks like this, with leopard-print tablecloths and lots of velvet throw pillows scattered around.
(Fig. 1.2)

I also have a little store attached to the café, where visitors can purchase top-of-the-line accordions and all of the *accoutrements* that go along with them (carrying cases, sheet music, rhinestone-studded bellows straps, etc.).

Kathy's Accordion Café is a successful venture and business is booming. The tables are always full, food and drink sales are through the roof (the "**Kenny Loggins** Latte" is a big favorite), and the adjoining store is performing well above expectations. However, despite the financial success I'm having, I don't have enough money to follow up on my next business venture—opening *another* Kathy's Accordion Café on the other side of town. I need to find a way to raise additional money, or **capital**, for the expansion.

There are different ways I could go looking for capital. One way is to get a loan from the bank. Since my first business is doing well, I should have no problem getting approved. I could ask for $100,000, get my cash, and then start working on my second location right away. But there are three things about the loan option that I don't like:

1. I have to pay the $100,000 back.
2. I have to make monthly payments on time, or risk having my café repossessed.
3. I have to pay interest *on top of* the $100,000.

The first part of that agreement, paying back the money I borrow, is not a surprise. Otherwise, it would be called "taking" money, or "accepting" money. But I'm a little nervous about taking on such a large amount of debt. I'll have to estimate what my future cash flow from the new store will be (which is just a best guess) to determine if I can afford the monthly payments. It feels tenuous and a little bit risky.

The second aspect of the loan, the possibility of losing my café, seems awfully severe, but the fact is that lenders are not known for being flexible when it comes to payments. The bank *might* do me the courtesy of contacting me the first time my payment is late, likely slapping on a late fee and/or other penalties. The second time I'm late (and this is if they're feeling generous), they might make a few calls and report me to the credit bureaus, making it harder (if not impossible) for me to borrow money in the future. After that, repossession of my business would be the next step. I'm reminded that I need to be *really certain* of my ability to pay back this loan or else I could lose everything that I've worked so hard to build.

The third part of the deal, interest, requires careful consideration. **Interest** is the extra fee I have to pay for borrowing money, usually expressed as a percentage of the total loan amount. Even seemingly small percentages can add up to huge fees over time, so I need to be able to look at the loan terms I am given and calculate my monthly payments as well as the total cost of the loan. Here are some samples:

NOTE: You can find any number of online calculators to figure out the interest payments on different loans, and I suggest you use them. That is how I got the calculations you'll see in these examples. Doing the calculations manually leaves a lot of room for errors, particularly when it comes to rounding.

Loan Sample 1:

My loan amount (or **principal**)	$100,000
My interest rate (or simply **rate**)	3% per year
My payback deadline (or **life of loan**)	5 years (or 60 months)
My payback terms (or **monthly payment**)	$1,796.87 monthly

If you take that monthly payment of $1,796.87 and multiply it by 60 months, you'll see that it comes to quite a bit more than $100,000. At the end of the five-year loan period, I will have paid a total of $107,812.14. That means it will cost me $7,812.14 in interest just to get access to that $100,000 loan.

Sometimes borrowers extend the life of a loan. This stretches out the payments over a longer period of time, which has the effect of lowering the monthly payment. Here's the same loan with the same interest rate calculated with a ten-year payback period.

Loan Sample 2:

Principal	$100,000
Rate	3% per year
Life of loan	10 years
Monthly payment	$965.61 monthly

Wow—stretching out the loan payment lowered my monthly payments by over $800. That could be a huge help to me if I'm having trouble making the payments every month. However, that approach only considers the short-term effects while ignoring the long-term costs. By paying less every month and taking an extra five years to pay off the loan, I have dramatically increased my cost of borrowing. At the end of ten years, I will have paid a total of $115,872.89. Doubling the life of the loan doubled the interest I had to pay.

These two loan samples, based on an interest rate of a mere 3%, represent a relatively low cost for borrowing. In the event that my interest rate is higher, let's say 6%, the numbers would look like this:

Loan Sample 3:

Principal	$100,000
Rate	6% per year
Life of loan	10 years
Monthly payment	$1,110.21 monthly

With this more realistic scenario, I will have paid a total of 33,224.60 in interest at the end of ten years. That's a third of the total amount I borrowed!

I get a little bummed out after studying these numbers and wish that there were some way for me to get the capital I need without having to pay it back. To my complete amazement, there is. All it takes is a little . . .

(Fig. 1.3)

I learn that I can get the $100,000 that I need by selling shares of Kathy's Accordion Café (KAC). Even better, I am under no obligation to pay back the people who contribute to my business by buying these shares.

Let that sink in a minute. I can ask for $100,000 from investors and then just *take* it. No complicated loan schedules, no pesky interest payments, and above all—no chance of getting my business repossessed.

If I decide to sell one share for $25, and I want to raise a total of $100,000, that means I'll have 4,000 shares available for sale. ($100,000/$25 = 4,000) Wouldn't it be great if I could find 100 interested buyers who would be willing to invest? If each of those 100 people bought 40 shares, it would look like this:

One investor: 40 shares x $25 = $1,000
One hundred investors each making that $1,000 investment
100 x $1,000 = $100,000. Done! Can it really be that easy?

No. Not really. That scenario is drastically oversimplified, but just go with it for the moment so we can take a look at the other side of this arrangement. Getting "free money" is a great deal for me, but what about the people who bought into my company? What can they actually *do* with a share of stock? After all, this is just a piece of paper we're talking about, right? (Right, except the market went digital ages ago and no one hands out paper stock certificates anymore.)

When I sell shares of KAC, I am actually selling pieces of the business itself. A person who buys my stock (even just one little share) becomes a **shareholder** and, by extension, a part owner in my business. Assuming that the second KAC location does as well as the first, I'll earn extra profits that I can share with these new owners. It will be my way of saying, "Here is your reward for buying into my business and believing in the transformative power of accordion music."

Giving this money to my shareholders is called a **dividend payment**. I can decide on any amount I want for the dividend. I could say that I'm going to pay $1.50 per share, which would give each investor a $60 windfall. (40 shares x $1.50 = $60) That may not sound like a great investment, but the dividend payments can always increase in amount and frequency. Plus, many companies continue to pay out dividends over time. My shareholders could make back the $1,000 they initially invested, and perhaps many multiples of that, as long as they hang on to the stock.

Funny thing about dividends, though—they aren't a requirement. I don't have to give out *any* dividends if I don't feel like it. Alternatively, I might toy with shareholders by giving out dividends one year, and then not paying them again for the next five years. That decision is entirely up to me. So while dividends can be a great way to make money, they aren't a reliable form of income.

This figure shows a satisfied stock market shareholder taking home some typical* dividends:

**Results not typical. Your dividends may differ.*

(Fig. 1.4)

There is another way to make money as a shareholder. When the price of a stock you own increases, you can sell the shares to someone else for the higher price and keep the profit. This is perhaps the most widely known (and widely romanticized) aspect of the stock market—the idea that a savvy investor can spot a winning company before anyone else does. Buying early when the share price is low means that you can cash in* later for big rewards.

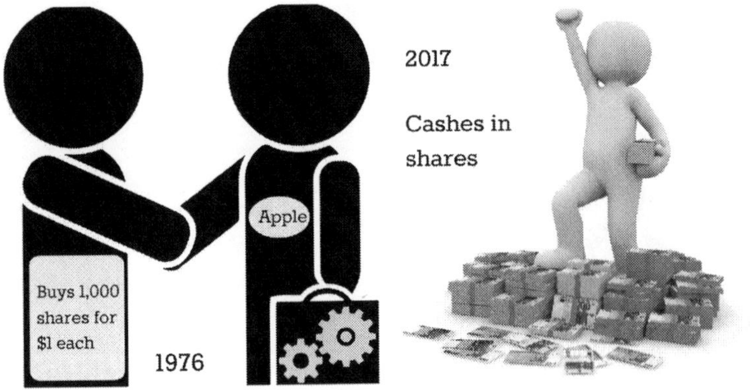

**Cash-in results not typical. Your cashing-in experience may differ.*
(Fig. 1.5)

When the price of a share increases, it is called **share appreciation**. Conversely, shares can ***depreciate*** as well.

Many, many things influence the price of a share of stock, and it would be impossible to discuss each and every one of them in the scope of this book. In general though, we can point to a few things. A successful business can usually sustain healthy share prices, especially if it can report good news to potential investors (a new CEO with a good track record or sales that surpassed expectations for the quarter). Companies with real problems, however, like a CEO that just got arrested for fraud or a product that tends to burst into flame, will have difficulty keeping share prices up.

Also, trends and hype play a role in the process. If shares of Kathy's Accordion Café jump from $25 to $100, many people may assume that this is a "hot stock" and they should buy in as well. When people see that shares of KAC are nearly sold out, it may create something of a furor and drive the prices up even *further*. Of course, this works in the opposite direction as well. Some shareholders see the price of a stock drop—even a tiny bit—and immediately bail out. This can start a panic that causes even *more* people to sell. As a result, the share price plunges.

The general state of the economy certainly plays a part in the prices of stocks. If people share a rosy outlook for the future, banking on the fact that the economy will grow and expand, then most will see this as a good time to invest in companies. If the outlook for the economy is poor, most businesses will be anticipating lower earnings and therefore, fewer people will want to invest in them.

Even with just this short case study, I'm betting that you have already figured out a great strategy to make money in the stock market. You just buy lots of shares of a promising company at rock-bottom prices, wait for the share price to increase, and then sell them at a massive profit. The ol' "Buy Low, Sell High" maxim. Well, that certainly happens for some people.

(Fig. 1.6)

But the reverse is possible as well. Your shares can drop in value and you're just out of luck–no returns, no do-overs.

(Fig. 1.7)

There are no guarantees in the stock market. Risk is the price of entry that investors pay for getting into the game.

But risk isn't something that only shareholders have to think about. Businesses that sell shares of their company to investors are taking a risk, too. I initially decided that I would sell shares of KAC because I wanted to raise $100,000 without having to pay it back. But I'm sure you know that there's no such thing as a free lunch. There has to be *some* kind of payback involved for KAC, right?

Vocabulary

Capital: Cash, plain and simple.

Dividend payment: A payment from a company to shareholders. The amount of the payment and the payment intervals are determined by the company.

Interest: The extra payment you make when you borrow money.

Life of loan: The amount of time you have to pay back money that you borrow.

Loggins, Kenny: Composer and singer of "This is It," one of my favorite songs from the K-Tel compilation album *Wings of Sound.* His duet with Journey frontman Steve Perry on "Don't Fight It" is pretty boss, too.

Monthly payment: The amount you pay every month to settle your debt with a lender. The monthly payment isn't just a fraction of the loan amount; it's a fraction of the loan plus interest.

Principal: The total amount of money that you borrow (without the interest added in).

Rate: The percentage used to calculate interest on a loan.

Shareholder: Anyone who buys shares of stock in a company. This term is often used interchangeably with *investor*. The terms aren't technically the same, because buying stock isn't the only way to invest in a business. (Someone might donate retail space to Kathy's Accordions, for example, in exchange for free accordion lessons. That would be a kind of investment.) For the purposes of this book however, they *will* be used interchangeably.

Share appreciation: When the price of a share of stock increases.

Share depreciation: When the price of a share of stock decreases.

Ain't Nothin' Free, Baby

My plan worked! Thanks to investors, Kathy's Accordion Café now has $100,000 to fund major projects such as opening a new store, acquiring more inventory, and commissioning a gilded statue of Weird Al Yankovic. (Trust me, gilding a statue is not cheap.) But the process of offering my stock for sale wasn't *nearly* as easy as I imagined it to be.

Since there is no requirement to pay back shareholders for their investment, and no requirement to pay dividends, KAC needed to do *something* to compensate the shareholders for the money they put up and the risk they took in buying my stock. I had to compensate them by giving them a say in how the business is run. (This wasn't my idea, by the way. Turns out that this is the law when you sell stock.)

Shareholders can't participate in the day-to-day aspects of running the business, but they *can* play a role in the company's major decisions. They can vote on candidates for the Board of Directors, for example, which means they have direct control over top management positions. They also get to vote on important agenda items. Topics up for discussion at a general meeting like acquiring another business, changing the structure of the company, or perhaps even executive-level compensation are all voted on by shareholders. Do you see how this could start cramping my style? I can't just *decide* to acquire a chain of bagpipe cafes, pay myself half a million dollars a year, or name my cat as the executive vice president. All of this has to be run by my shareholders first.

I also have to keep my shareholders up to date on the company's financial standing through constant reporting. I am required to provide them with a complete accounting of my activities by submitting paperwork like balance sheets, cash flow records, and profit and loss statements on a regular basis. That's my trade-off for accepting their money.

Compare this method of generating capital to simply borrowing money. While I didn't like the idea of making interest payments or risking repossession of my business, I now realize that the *benefit* of borrowing money is that the bank doesn't want to have a hand in my operations. Once I get the money from them, I can be selling accordions one day and Ginsu knives the next—they don't really care.

That might be a wee exaggeration, but you get the point, right? They just want to be paid on time.

Bank Loan PROS	**Issuing Stock PROS**
After the bank gives me the money, I don't have to keep justifying my business to them.	I don't have to pay the money back to investors.
Bank Loan CONS	**Issuing Stock CONS**
I have to pay high interest rates. I can have my business taken away if I'm late with payments.	Other people have a say in how I run my business. I have to constantly provide transparent reports to shareholders.

Do you see the writing on the wall now? *Getting* money means *giving something* in return. As the owner of KAC, I had an important decision to make. What exactly would I give up to get the capital I needed for expansion?

In my case, selling shares of stock was the best fit because I was uncertain about the future profitability of my second store (at least in the short term). I didn't want to lock myself into a payment agreement with a lender, so I accepted the outside influence that shareholders brought in exchange for their cash. This is a big decision to make, and it's not the right choice for every business. That's why some companies don't sell stock shares (meaning that they remain **private companies**) and others do (meaning they become **public companies**).

But even after I made the decision to go public, I still had some big questions that I needed to answer. The main one was how, exactly I would go about selling those shares. Could I just print up some certificates and sell them at my café along with a Loggins Latte and a **Pablo Cruise** Croissant?

You know what makes it a Pablo Cruise croissant? The JAM.

(Fig. 2.1)

I wish! I found out that KAC needed to jump through some bureaucratic hoops first.

Vocabulary

Pablo Cruise: Soft rockin' band that dominated AM radio in the 1970s. "Love Will Find a Way" was a big hit. Posed mostly naked on the cover of their album *Lifeline* 'cause that used to be a thing. (See also: Orleans)

Private companies: Companies that do not sell shares of stock to raise money. They rely on their own operations to generate profits and additional capital.

Public companies: Companies that raise funds by selling shares of their stock to the public.

The SEC Is the Boss of Me

Before I could start selling off pieces of KAC, I had to officially apply to the government agency in charge of overseeing the stock market. The process was fraught with paperwork and . . . well, mostly **paperwork. Crap tons** of it, in fact. The government agency in charge of this paperwork is the Securities and Exchange Commission, or **SEC**.

(Fig. 3.1)

This federal agency serves as the watchdog of the stock market. Before I could open my business up to public trading, the SEC performed an extensive and thorough background check on KAC. They examined my management structure, looked at my bookkeeping records, considered how much debt I was carrying—basically, they conducted all of the research necessary to assure investors that Kathy's Accordion Café was a verifiable business. (But keep in mind that "verifying" isn't the same as "endorsing." Approval from the SEC only means that my company is legitimate; it doesn't mean that it is a particularly good investment.)

All of those details were recorded on the SEC's FORM S-1, the registration statement. When the SEC officially approved the registration statement, then my application was declared "effective," meaning that shares could be sold. Woo hoo! Time to open the bubbly!

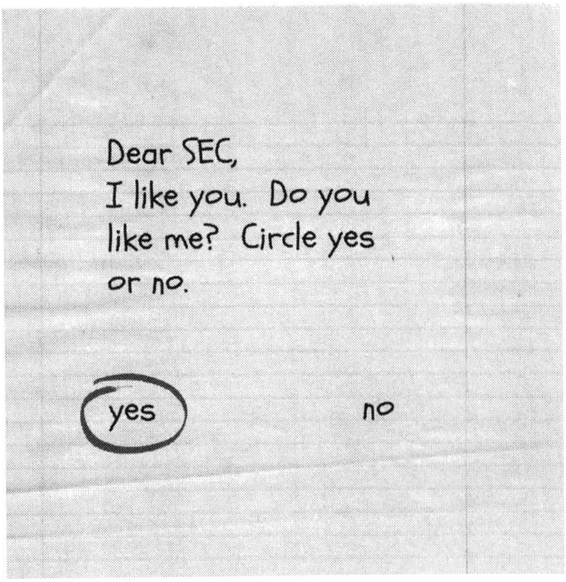

This is what the application process would look like if it were up to me.
(Fig. 3.2)

But after popping the champagne, I had to settle back down, because I realized that I would be *continually* proving myself to the SEC through other forms of reporting. For example, form 8-K is for current reports, Form 10-Q is for quarterly reports, and Form 10-K is for the annual report. (And these are just the main ones!) This reporting system allows the SEC to keep tabs on me even after my initial vetting. If they have cause to think there are a bunch of **shenanigans** going on over at KAC (insider trading, accounting fraud, false or misleading information), then I could be in trouble.

What kind of trouble? Well, since the SEC allowed me into the market in the first place, they can also take me right out of it. And that's just the beginning of the troubles! While the federal government takes the primary role in prosecution, states have their own laws as well. Depending on the severity of the offense, punishments can range from civil (usually paying a fine) to criminal (paying *really* big fines plus prison). But this oversight is necessary—investors rely on this service so they know that the companies they invest in are on the level.

In fact, the SEC is an agency born of necessity. In 1929, after the market crash, the American people were downright terrified to invest in stocks. Who could blame them? The crash ushered in the Great Depression, an era of high unemployment, low wages, and a stagnant economy. However, functioning markets help grease the wheels of the economy, and the United States needed to get back on its feet. In an effort to convince the American people that they could trust the markets once again, President Franklin D. Roosevelt established the Securities and Exchange Commission. This office would be responsible for assuring potential investors that companies were properly investigated before their stock shares were offered for sale. (I'm sure that many folks would appreciate a similar agency to regulate online dating sites.)

Once KAC had the blessing of the SEC, then my shares were ready to offer to investors. That was very good news. It was a lot of work to get KAC ready for a public sale, and I was ready to make some money. All I had to do next was figure out where I would sell them.

That part was actually quite easy. Like most other things that you buy, stocks are sold in a store.

Vocabulary

Paperwork, crap tons: Finding paperwork in the "crap ton" form happens all the time. If you've ever itemized your taxes, applied for a mortgage, or filled out a FAFSA form, you have experienced a crap ton of paperwork. In this instance, the crap tons of paperwork refer to the reports that a company submits to the SEC in order to become (and remain) a publicly traded stock.

SEC: The Securities and Exchange Commission, a governmental agency that oversees the stock market. Its role is to investigate companies *before* they are available to the public to ensure that they are legitimate businesses. It continues to keep tabs on companies by requiring regular reports from them.

Shenanigans: A whole bunch of silliness or nonsense. Sometimes it can be harmless, like when you loosen the lid of the salt shaker or do the "pull my finger" trick. Other times, it can be nefarious in nature, like misrepresenting a business or falsifying documents to the SEC. For the record, I am in favor of *all* shenanigans that are within the realm of the law.

(Ex) ch-ch-ch-ch-ch-ch-CHANGES!

A **stock exchange** is basically a store that sells stocks. The United States is so important in the world of stock trading that it has two stores, or exchanges, for selling stock. There's the New York Stock Exchange, or **NYSE**, and the **NASDAQ** Exchange.

In order to sell KAC stock, I had to appeal directly to one of the stock exchanges and seek permission to be added to the "store." (Guess what? This process also involved a crap ton of paperwork.) When the exchange agreed to offer my company stock for sale, then Kathy's Accordion Café was officially "**listed**."

Here are some important facts about these exchanges:

The New York Stock Exchange

(Fig. 4.1)

The NYSE is the oldest of the exchanges, established in 1817. It has around 2,800 listings, including many established, quintessentially American companies like Coca-Cola, IBM, and General Electric. It is the largest exchange in the world in terms of value. The last figure I could find on the total value of the companies listed on the NYSE was $21.1 trillion.

The NASDAQ Exchange

(Fig. 4.2)

The NASDAQ Exchange is really new to the game—it didn't open until 1971. NASDAQ stands for "National Association of Securities Dealers Automatic Quotations." (You will probably never remember that acronym after you finish reading this paragraph and that's just fine.) As the first *automated* stock exchange, it eliminated the need for hordes of traders screaming at each other on the floor. With NASDAQ—get this—you could just phone in your order. Now that's what I call progress.

The NASDAQ lists over 3,800 companies (quite a bit more than the NYSE) and has a higher volume of trading. In spite of this, the total value of NASDAQ stocks only comes to about $11 trillion—much less than the

NYSE. It's also thought of as the tech exchange—it counts Cisco, Intel, Oracle, and Sun Microsystems among its listings.

(Incidentally, other countries have their own exchanges too. The United Kingdom has the London Stock Exchange, Japan has the Tokyo Stock Exchange, Canada has the Toronto Stock exchange, and so forth. But the NYSE and the NASDAQ are the largest exchanges in the world.)

You may have heard the terms "**stock market**" and "**stock exchange**" used interchangeably, but there is a big difference between them. A "stock exchange" refers to a distinct entity that serves as the link between stock shares, buyers, and sellers. "The stock market" is a general term that discusses how *all* of the stocks (on both of the exchanges) are currently faring. That is, are most of them trending up or down? Are prices good or bad? Is it a good time to buy or not? Nothing specific—just a general measure.

Here's a little vocabulary substitution exercise to further clarify the difference between a stock market and a stock exchange.

> ***Me:*** *"I'm going to <u>Wool-Mart</u> today to buy the Richard Simmons DVD "<u>Sweatin' to the Oldies</u>."*
>
> ***You:*** *"Good idea! <u>Prices</u> are good at Wool-Mart right now."*
>
> "Wool-Mart" is the store, "Sweatin' to the Oldies" is the product, and "prices" refer to all prices at that store in a general way. By substituting the underlined words and replacing them with market vocabulary, we can make the same observation about a possible Wall Street transaction.
>
> ***Me:*** *"I'm going to the <u>stock exchange</u> today to buy some shares of <u>Coca-Cola</u>."*
>
> ***You:*** *"Good idea! The <u>stock market</u> is doing great right now. I bet those shares will be worth a lot someday!"*

In this example, the "stock exchange" is the store where the buying will take place, Coca-Cola is the product, and the "stock market" refers to the general price trends in all stocks.

While we're discussing investment products, this is a good time for me to revisit my policy on giving stock advice. Although I am often asked about this, I shy away from the practice. I'm about *educating* people, not steering them in any particular direction. For that reason, I will offer no guidance on which is the better investment—Richard Simmons DVDs or Coca-Cola. (I *will* say that Warren Buffett is heavily invested in both of them, though.)

These are big-league investment decisions right here.
(Fig. 4.3)

The first time that a stock is offered for sale on an exchange is a very, very big deal. In fact, it has its own fancy acronym that you will learn about next. Dropping market-related acronyms into casual conversation is a great way to start showing off your newly-acquired finance knowledge. I suggest you follow the next chapter closely and find ways to work this new vocabulary into small talk.

Vocabulary

Listed: Refers to a company being added to a stock exchange so that shares of its stock are available for sale to the public.

NASDAQ: One of the two stock exchanges in the United States, the National Association of Securities Dealers Automatic Quotations. It has a large number of tech stocks in its listings.

NYSE: One of two stock exchanges in the United States, the New York Stock Exchange. It mainly lists the stocks of older, established companies.

Stock exchange: A specific entity that deals in the buying and selling of stocks.

Stock market: A general reference to activity that takes place in the stock exchanges. It is usually a commentary on price trends, such as, "It's a good time to invest in the stock market." Or it could be commentary on the very idea of investing, as in, "The stock market scares me. That's why I keep my money in empty Nutella jars."

Hi-Ho, Hi-Ho, to IPO We Go . . .

IPO stands for "Initial Public Offering." The IPO is a unique event because it is the one and only time that investors can buy stock shares on the **primary market**. That is, they are buying the shares directly from the stock exchange.

Some investors are very big into buying shares during an IPO, but I think that approach is rarely justified. It reminds me of those people who camp out on a sidewalk for days on end to buy a new tech gadget. They go to all that trouble to pay top dollar for a product that will drop in price in just a few months. Even if the price doesn't drop, said gadget can often be easily procured by just strolling into the store and buying one after the hype dies down. And here's a fun stock fact—history has shown that IPOs usually operate the same way. There really aren't a lot of instances where buying stock during an IPO ended up being a significant advantage for the buyer. We'll just have to put all of this down to the fact that some people like being early adopters.

Online marketplace Alibaba certainly had a lot of early adopters clamoring to buy its stock shares. When the company held its IPO in 2014, it raised an eye-popping $25 billion. The share price wasn't even very expensive at $68 a pop, but when you sell around 368 million shares, the money really starts to pile up.

Alibaba was able to raise this astronomical sum because the company had already proven its worth. It was able to show, through detailed financial reporting, that it had maintained and steadily increased its profits over the past several years. This wasn't an accident or dumb luck. The Alibaba team conducted extensive market research, scrutinized its competitors, and devised a strategic long-term plan that would ensure its future success. As the sports commentators like to say, "They came to *play*."

This sound financial record made Alibaba a very attractive prospect for the marketplace and therefore, a high **valuation**, or estimate of total worth, was placed on the business. This high valuation, in turn, generated a lot of excitement and interest in the company. The excitement and interest churned up into full-fledged hype, and by the time the IPO happened, people were practically lobbing fistfuls of dollar bills onto the steps of the NYSE just to buy some shares.

This sequence of events is the perfect and most reliable way to launch a company into the public sector. It follows this simple three-step plan:

1. Demonstrate worth through impressive financial records.
2. Create excitement for investors and generate some hype.
3. Hold IPO and collect the money.

Alibaba's IPO was a huge success[1]—but not every IPO story has a happy ending. Sometimes, companies decide to skip step one entirely and go straight for the hype in step two. Instead of providing financial records that show their stellar past and current performance, they insist that the company will prove its worth sometime in the future. This is shaky ground; instead of relying on facts, the investors are left to rely on projections.

You may find it hard to believe that investors would want to hand over money to a company without a successful track record (or any track record, for that matter), but it happens more often than you think. There were lots of instances of this back in the days when the dot.com bubble was growing and any chump with a modem and Windows 95 was suddenly an Internet entrepreneur. Even logical and thoughtful investors got carried away and bought handfuls of magic beans from slick-talking dot.com salesmen.

Take the case of pets.com, an online business that sold and shipped pet supplies anywhere in the United States. They came roaring onto the scene in 1998 by hammering away at step two: generating hype. Their marketing method, though a bit unorthodox, was surprisingly successful. They used a sock puppet.

You used to be able to launch an IPO by doing this. The 90s were a crazy time.
(Fig. 5.1)

The pets.com dog was a no-frills puppet. He was made from an ordinary tube sock and had his ears pinned into place. The puppeteer made no attempt to create any semblance of theatrical illusion, which meant his arm was usually visible in photographs or spotted bobbing up and down in videos. This tongue-in-cheek approach really seemed to resonate with viewers, and the company's popularity grew.

Pets.com commercials dominated the airwaves. The puppet was often shown "interviewing" pets about the shipments of food, toys, and specialty collars that they had just received. But additionally, he sang, told jokes, and generally yukked it up until he became something of a celebrity in his own right. He was a guest on *Good Morning America*, he was interviewed for *People* magazine, and he even made an appearance as a giant balloon in the Macy's Thanksgiving Day Parade. Pets.com paid $1.2 million for a Super Bowl ad that was wildly successful, in part due to its clever tag line: "Because pets can't drive." It seemed that the business had everything going for it. Everything, that is, except for profits.

The folks at pets.com made some blunders that will live on in stock market lore, all filed under the category of "what NOT to do when you launch a business." In fact, if we refer back to that simple list of three things that responsible companies do when they are getting ready for an IPO, it is easy to see where they made their biggest mistakes.

1. **Demonstrate worth through impressive financial records.**
   During its first fiscal year, pets.com earned revenues of $619,000 while spending $11.8 million on advertising. This contrast didn't suggest that the company had a solid earnings plan in place.
2. **Create excitement for investors and generate some hype.**
   OK, this one they managed to pull off. There's nothing wrong with being really good at step two, as long as you didn't skip step one to get there. *Oops.*
3. **Hold IPO and collect the money.**
   They managed to accomplish this as well by taking in an impressive $82 million after going public. The only problem was that, as I mentioned earlier, taking money from investors means giving them something in return. Most investors like to see their companies earn impressive profits and hand out morale-boosting dividends. They also hope that share prices continually rise so the value of their investment increases. Did any of these things happen?

Nope. The company folded nine months later.

I know that things always seem clearer in hindsight, but really, I'm not sure why investors didn't ask more questions or insist on seeing detailed sales plans. For example, the pets.com approach to entice new customers by offering reduced prices and free shipping was not a sustainable practice. I don't think you need an MBA to do that kind of math:

Cost to acquire 1 unit dog kibble:	-$15
Sale Price:	$12
Shipping Cost:	-$8
Our profit	-$11

And the worst part of that plan is, the more you sell, the *further* you go into debt!

Of course, few people would argue that the above plan was a long-term solution for making money. The folks at pets.com accepted these initial losses as the cost of doing business and reasoned that they would eventually turn a profit because their loyal customer base would start to order more frequently and buy more expensive products. However, a market analysis (which they apparently didn't bother to conduct) would have shown otherwise. In spite of the favorable prices and free shipping, consumers just weren't ready to make a regular habit of ordering pet supplies online. They continued using their tried-and-true method—picking up pet supplies while they were doing their own brick-and-mortar shopping—and pets.com ascended to that great stock exchange in the sky.

When it came time to get ready for my own IPO, I took that story to heart and regarded it as a cautionary tale. I couldn't just assume that success was inevitable; I had to have actual *proof* based on financial records, marketing reports, demographic studies, and other research that would help me make an accurate prediction for KAC's future. Once I had established that, I could move on to the "hype" aspect. (Luckily, I was able to convince Weird Al to come by the store for the unveiling of the gilded statue out front. That man has an incredibly dedicated following.)

After all of that build up, the only thing left to do was announce my IPO date and hope for the best. The result? Thanks to careful planning and a can't-miss concept, I sold all of my KAC shares and raised enough money to fund my second location. Imagine! All that, and I didn't even need to use a wacky mascot or a silly sock puppet to advertise my stock. (Come to think of it though, some might argue that Weird Al could fit into either of those categories.)

For people who didn't manage to buy into KAC during the IPO, they still have a chance to invest in the business. All they have to do is wait until a KAC shareholder decides to sell some shares of the stock. They can then acquire the shares "second hand" from these sellers. For that reason, this is called trading on the **secondary market**, and it is really where the majority of stock buying and selling takes place. Buyers and sellers don't interact directly though; they use a stock exchange as a middleman to service the transactions.

Going public isn't the best course of action for every business. While the "cash up front" aspect of holding an IPO is certainly exciting, being a publicly-held company can bring with it special challenges and frustrations. Likewise, investors need to exercise caution when they purchase shares and become part owners in a business. Not every business will be profitable, after all, and some will be complete clunkers. By reviewing the potential risks and rewards for all of the market participants in this chart, you'll see that it is a perfectly balanced system. Each side must take a certain leap of faith in order to get access to financial opportunity.

Stock Issuing PROS	**Stock Buying PROS**
I get the capital that I need to start my expansion project.	The buyer has a share of stock that could increase in price. It could then be sold for a profit.
I am under no obligation to pay back the money to investors.	The buyer can get dividends.

Stock Issuing CONS	Stock Buying CONS
I have to jump through a lot of regulatory hoops to issue my stock.	If the stock price falls, the buyer is just out of luck.
I have to constantly report to my shareholders about the business, and I have to give them a say in how it is run.	The buyer may never get dividends.

You've just completed the first section of the book, and you've already learned some important fundamentals. You understand the rationale behind a company "going public" and the implications of that decision. You know a bit about the administrative process required when transforming from a private company to a public company, such as applying to the SEC and preparing for regular reporting and constant oversight. And finally, you've got some technical vocabulary under your belt that will be useful as you continue to learn about basic market mechanics. Why not try your hand at the first quiz to commemorate this achievement?

[1]*Actually, it wasn't the success it was made out to be. Even after making $25 billion on opening day, Alibaba co-founder Jack Ma said, "If I had another life, I would keep my company private." (Egan, 2015) Now really, what could make someone regret a multi-billion dollar windfall? The trade-off. The increased scrutiny from "investors, regulators, and the media" drove him crazy. Really, he should have talked to me first. I could have sent him my "Ain't Nothin' Free, Baby" chapter (for a nominal fee), and he would have had a better idea of what he was getting himself into.*

Vocabulary

IPO: Initial Public Offering. This is the first time that a company's stock is available for sale to the public. IPOs are often surrounded by a lot of hype, especially the IPOs of large companies like Facebook or Snapchat.

Primary market: The market in which buyers purchase stock directly from the stock exchange. This kind of sale only happens during IPOs.

Secondary market: The market in which most stocks are bought and sold, whereby shares are exchanged between buyers and sellers.

Valuation: How much a company is worth. This is often a best guess. If the valuation is based on the company's successful history and impressive earnings, it is probably a sound valuation. If it is a valuation based on projections, it is shaky at best.

QUIZ 1

1. What is a share of stock?
    a. Part ownership of a company
    b. Part of a company's cash flow
    c. Part ownership of a company's merchandise
    d. Part of a company's earnings

2. What are the two ways you can make money owning stock?
    a. The stock value increases; the company is sold
    b. The company pays dividends; the value of the stock increases
    c. The company sells more shares of stock; private investors buy shares
    d. The company is sold; the company issues dividends

3. Which of these things is needed to expand a business?
    a. Cannoli
    b. Capitol
    c. Capital
    d. Carbon

4. The SEC made it safe for investors to put their money into the stock market after the Great Depression.
    a. True
    b. False

5. Which of the following is a likely reason that a business would avoid getting a loan?
    a. The bank's interest rates are too low.

b. The bank's application process is too easy.
c. The bank is clear across town and traffic is terrible during business hours.
d. The company doesn't want debt.

6. When a company sells stock, it is not required to pay back its investors.

a. True
b. False

7. The SEC is the organization that oversees publicly traded companies. What does the SEC stand for?

a. Security Exchange Conference
b. Securities and Exchange Commission
c. Simian Evolution and Conversion
d. Securities, Enterprises, and Companies

8. The two stock exchanges in the United States are:

a. Wall Street and the New York Stock Exchange
b. Wall Street and NASDAQ
c. NASDAQ and New York Stock Exchange
d. NYSE and Dow Jones

9. Which exchange has more tech stocks listed?

a. NASDAQ
b. Wall Street
c. Dow Jones Industrial Average
d. New York Stock Exchange

10. Which stock exchange is the oldest?

a. NYSE
b. S&P 500
c. Warren Buffett
d. Wall Street

11. The difference between the stock market and a stock exchange is:
    a. Only stock brokers can use the stock exchange; anyone has access to the stock market
    b. The stock exchange is automated; the stock market isn't
    c. The stock market refers to the market in general; the stock exchange is where stocks are bought and sold
    d. The stock market is where stocks are bought and sold; the stock exchange is a general term.

12. On a scale of 1-10, how awesome is Richard Simmons?
    a. 5
    b. 8
    c. 9
    d. anything 11 and above

13. How are shareholders compensated for the risk they take when they buy stock?
    a. They earn dividends when the company earns a profit.
    b. They influence business decisions that the company makes by voting.
    c. Both A and B
    d. None of these

14. You can lower your monthly loan payments by extending the life of your loan.
    a. True
    b. False

15. Why would an investor choose to invest his money in a business?
    a. It guarantees future earnings.
    b. It is a risk-free investment.
    c. It offers the chance to serve on the board of the company.
    d. It offers the possibility of future earnings.

Answer Key for Quiz 1

1. A

   While choice "D" is really close, it doesn't go far enough. The share means you actually own part of the entire business, not just its earnings.

2. B

   If you are a lucky shareholder, you'll experience both dividends and increases in value, though neither one of those is guaranteed.

3. C

   If you confused "capital" and "capitol," I suggest you go look up the difference. People will judge you for that.

4. B

   The SEC was created so that businesses would be properly vetted before offering their stock for public sale. While this service improved investor confidence, saying that it made investing "safe" is going too far. The word "safe" suggests that investing is risk-free, and we all know that's not the case.

5. D

   Interest rates are never too low and applications are never too easy. In my own case, driving across town in traffic might *also* be a reason to avoid applying for a loan, but "D" is still the better choice.

6. A

   That's one of the perks of selling stock to raise money.

7. B

   While learning acronyms can be a pain, this one is pretty important.

8. C

   Wall Street is where the NYSE is located, FYI. The NASDAQ offices are in Times Square.

9. A

   If you missed this one, don't worry. As soon as you start following the stock market in the news, it will be easy to commit to memory.

10. A

    Warren Buffett though? (Snicker)

11. C

    Remember, an "exchange" is just a store. "The market" is a general term.

12. D

    That's right. "D" is the correct answer and nothing else.

13. B

    Answer "A" may have thrown you, but that is not the correct choice because dividends are never guaranteed—even if the company records a profit. Companies decide when and if they distribute dividends, and they base that decision on many factors, not just profits.

14. A

    This is true, but you should consider the additional long-term costs.

15. D

    Make sure you clarify that those future earnings are *possible* and not *guaranteed*, as stated in choice "A."

Congratulations—you completed your first quiz. You may have discovered that in order to earn a perfect score, you have to give Richard Simmons the recognition that I feel he deserves. That's just one of the perks of writing your own book.

If you were able to answer all of these questions, then you have successfully activated your Market Mojo. Don't stop now! Keep feeding the beast by moving on to section two.

Part 2

Understanding Indices

How Now, Dow Jones?
The S&P 500 Conundrum
Got Nasdaq?
You Give Me Fever

Understanding Indices

Understanding what an **index** is will be central to your overall understanding of the market. The first lesson you need to get under your belt is that the plural for "index" is "**indices**." Isn't that fun? (You will see "indexes" all the time in print and online. I recommend that you write to these publications and complain vociferously.) While there are several words that follow this pattern (matrix, appendix, helix) the –ix ending can also be used to show that the noun in question refers to a female.

Amelia Earhart was an aviatrix.

(Fig. 6.1)

The executrix has the legal responsibility to carry out the instructions in this will. (Fig. 6.2)

Actually, the use of –ix as a female indicator is quite antiquated and rarely used today. But because *dominatrix* is one of the few forms still in circulation, the -ix ending has become a naughty suffix of sorts. (Who says grammar can't be sexy?) For example, a Google image search for the entirely respectable professions of "editrix" and "administratrix" will turn up some really (ahem) interesting photos that licensing and good taste and licensing prevent me from reprinting here.

In the case of the stock market, an index is simply a list of stocks. Having stocks organized into lists makes it easier to determine how the market is doing at a glance. For example, if you want a general indicator of how the market is faring today, you probably don't want to look up the movements of every stock on the exchanges, chart their gains or losses, and then average those numbers yourself. You (like everyone else) would much rather have a faster and easier way to get that information, right?

The indices do that for you. They group together certain kinds of stocks so you can get an idea of how all stocks are doing, or how stocks in specific industries are doing. This section of the book will explain the "Big Three" indices (The Dow Jones Industrial Average, The S&P 500, and the NASDAQ) so you know what each of them represent.

All of these indices report something different to investors, so no single index should be used in isolation. Rather, they should *all* be consulted to give a broader, and thus more realistic, portrait of general market conditions.

How Now, Dow Jones?

Near the end of the nineteenth century, Charles Dow, co-creator of the firm Dow & Co. (the same company that created the Wall Street Journal), published a list of twelve companies that he considered vital to the economy. It wasn't what you would call a diversified list; there were ten railroads and two industrial firms. He took the current selling price for one share of each of the stocks, added them together, and then divided by twelve.

Ten railroads = $10 a share
Total = $100

Industrial firm 1 = $18 a share
Industrial firm 2 = $16 a share
Total = $34

Grand total = $134

$134/12 stocks = $11.17 per share average

Seriously???? That's all you have to do to have your own index and have your name live on forever in stock market history? Add twelve numbers and find the average of them?

Charles Dow, father of the hipster beard trend.
(Fig. 7.1)

Later on, the composition of the list was changed. Railroads got their own index, called "The Dow Jones Railroad Average" (now known as "The Dow Jones Transportation Average"). Industries were separated out and known thereafter as "The Dow Jones Industrial Average."

The Dow Jones Industrial Average ("**DJIA**" or just "The Dow" from this point forward) went on to increase the number of companies on its list to 30—a number that is still maintained today. Although the DJIA doesn't follow specific criteria for inclusion, its companies are generally considered to be the heavy hitters of American companies. You can look at the list and easily see that's the case.

Companies on the DJIA		
3M	American Express	Apple
Boeing	Caterpillar	Chevron
Cisco	Coca-Cola	DuPont
Exxon	General Electric	Goldman Sachs
Home Depot	Intel	IBM
Johnson & Johnson	J. P. Morgan Chase	McDonalds
Merck	Microsoft	Nike
Pfizer	Proctor & Gamble	Travelers
United Health Group	United Technologies	Verizon
Visa	Wal-Mart	Disney

Here's the breakdown of **sectors**, or different industries on the Dow.

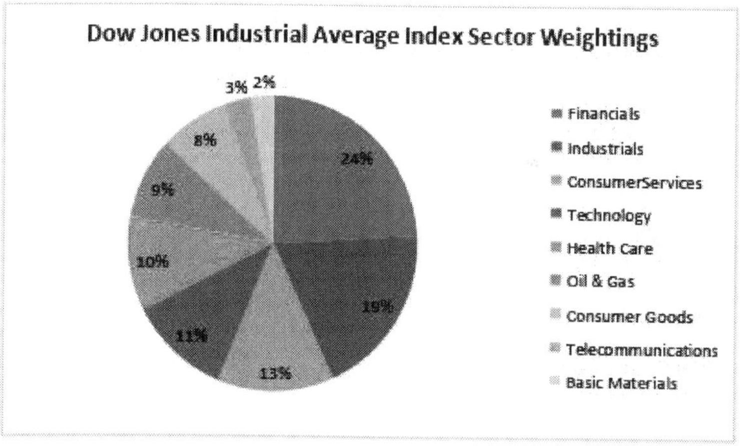

(Fig 7.2)

The companies on the Dow are known as "**blue chip stocks**," a term you may have heard bandied about in stock-talk circles. A blue chip is nothing complicated—it's basically a big, well-known stock that has a history of steady earnings and is considered stable bet for the future.

The composition of the companies on the Dow changes periodically to ensure that they continue to represent a profitable cross-section of the current market. For example, Bethlehem Steel, one of the largest American producers of steel, was a mainstay of the Dow for decades. But when cheaper steel became available elsewhere, the company eventually folded and was removed from the list.

Sears is another good example. The company was the king of retail back in its day, but fortunes change. Despite their velour sweaters, Toughskins jeans, and three-piece polyester suits, they became less profitable over the years and were eventually removed from the Dow.

I'm sure that you have seen reports about the Dow on the news. You might see something like, "The Dow Jones Industrial Average closed at 18,641.03 today." Or maybe you just see the movement of the index, as in, "The Dow Jones is up 80 points from yesterday."

Do these numbers mean anything to you? Or do you tend to react like this?

"The Dow Jones Industrial Average closed at 18,641.03 today."

(Fig. 7.3)

"The Dow Jones is up 80 points from yesterday."

"Blah, blah, Dow Jones, blah, blah numbers blah."

Well, now we are going to learn about all of these numbers so you can react to stock quotes with actual expressions. Get ready to *emote.*

Today's DJIA is a **price-weighted index**, which is a very different system from Charles Dow's original mean average. To determine an overall value for the DJIA, we first take the price of one share of each stock on the list and total them up. I'll use a small index—one with just five companies—to show how this works:

Monday

Stock	Price
Apple	$20
Banana	$20
Cantaloupe	$20
Durian	$20
Eggplant	$20
TOTAL	$100

On the following day, suppose you hear that the total value of the index is $90. You'd know that there was a drop in share prices, but you wouldn't have any details. You wouldn't know if just one stock lost $10 in value, or if multiple stocks lost a combined total of $10. You'd have to look at the index and read the share prices for the individual companies to be sure. In this case, a quick scan of the index shows that Tuesday's drop in value can be attributed to Eggplant moving from $20 to $10.

Tuesday

Stock	Price
Apple	$20
Banana	$20
Cantaloupe	$20
Durian	$20
Eggplant	$10
TOTAL	$90

The total dollar value of the index, then, gives a general indicator of how all of the stocks on the list are doing. To find out which companies are driving the change, you can check the prices of individual stocks. With a list of just 30 stocks, that's not so difficult to do. So why does the DJIA have to muck everything up by reporting in points? (Points that, I might add, seem to have absolutely no relation to the dollar value that is reported.)

The points are needed because companies often go up or down in value for reasons other than their operations or profitability. They might experience a merger or a takeover. They may spin off one of their divisions into a separate company. They may issue dividends that were much higher or lower than expected. All of these events can temporarily change a company's stock price in a way that isn't necessarily reflective of its true value. The point system aims to make allowances for these events and therefore report a more accurate number for the index.

We'll take a detour here for an in-depth look at one of the most common events that distort the value of an index, the "**stock split**." Once you understand how splits work, the point system will make sense to you.

Stock Splits

Occasionally, companies will offer their stock for sale at a deep discount. They do so to make the price of the stock more affordable and encourage new investors. Maybe you've been saving up for a share of Eggplant but you aren't able to get the $20 that you need to buy it. But if Eggplant's stock splits, the price of one share is cut in half. Now it only costs $10 to buy into Eggplant. This is great news for you—you can now get in the game.

1 share costs $10

(Fig. 7.4)

(Fig. 7.5)

But what about this guy?

1 share cost $20, 5 shares cost $100

(Fig. 7.6)

He's a little cheesed off because he saved like crazy to buy five shares of Eggplant at $20 each. *Now* he finds out that if he had just waited a little longer, he could have gotten them for half price. Is there any justice for this guy?

There is. Current shareholders are compensated after a stock split by having their shares *doubled.* That means that the guy who had five shares now suddenly owns ten.

(Fig. 7.7)

This is called a two-for-one stock split. The company doubles the number of existing shares and *simultaneously* cuts the share price by half.

That's just one way to use the stock split formula. Offering a three-for-one stock split would mean *tripling* the number of existing shares and cutting the share price to *one third* of the original. There are plenty of four-for-one stock splits out there, too. A very famous stock split took place in June of 2014, when Apple made headlines for its seven-for-one stock split. Its shares, trading at just over $700, were sold for $92.69 after the split took effect, and the current investors had their holdings multiplied by seven.

The most important thing to realize about stock splits, though, is that they are something of an illusion. That's because the *value* of the shares doesn't change at all—just the number of them does. Think of it this way—I usually have a pizza for lunch that I cut into four slices. If I suddenly decide to cut the same pizza into eight slices one day, it doesn't mean that I have *more* pizza. It just means that I divided it differently, right?

It's the same idea with stock splits. If you think about the guy who had five shares turn into ten, all he really has is more pieces of paper in his hand. The total value of his shares *before* the split was $100 (5 shares X $20 each). The total value of his shares *after* the split is *still* $100 (10 shares X $10 each).

Again, announcing a stock split is a way for Eggplant to get some publicity, drive up interest in the stock, and get more people to invest. By lowering the cost of stock shares in proportion to the additional shares offered to existing shareholders, the company has a great way to entice new investment while keeping the *value* of the stock intact. When Eggplant stock drops its price from $20 to $10 after announcing a two-for-one stock split, we now know that the price didn't really "drop." It just *changed.*

The DJIA needs to figure out how it can clarify the difference between a price *dropping* (price is lower because a share is worth less) and a price *changing* (price is lowered by the company as part of an economic strategy like a stock split). This isn't as hard as it sounds, but you may want to get a calculator and do the work with me.

We'll use the same simplified index as before, which is valued at $100 on Monday.

Monday

Stock	Price
Apple	$20
Banana	$20
Cantaloupe	$20
Durian	$20
Eggplant	$20
TOTAL	$100

On Tuesday the index is affected by Eggplant's two-for-one stock split.

Tuesday

Stock	Price
Apple	$20
Banana	$20
Cantaloupe	$20
Durian	$20
Eggplant	$10
TOTAL	$90

Tuesday's index is calculated at $90 total, but this isn't an accurate reflection of the value of the index. Remember—the Eggplant stock didn't "drop" to $10 a share. Eggplant purposely changed the price of the stock to accommodate a two-for-one split. While the value of Eggplant stock is still the same, the $10 share price and the $90 valuation of the total index don't reflect that fact. We have to find some way to show what is really going on. Basically, we need to make Tuesday's $90 valuation look like $100 to anyone who is following the index. (If that seems confusing, think back to the pizza example. Monday's prices show a pizza cut into eight slices. Tuesday's prices show the same exact pizza cut into four slices. We need to make sure people understand that even though the number of slices is smaller, there is still the same amount of pizza on Tuesday as there was on Monday.)

We can do this using the **Dow divisor**. The Dow divisor is a special number that translates stock prices to stock points. The points ensure that the index reports the size of the pizza, not the number of slices. Here is a super-simplified example of how the Dow divisor is calculated.

Begin by assigning points to the Monday prices—that will give us a baseline. We know that the value of the five companies added up to $100. We can just divide $100 by five to come up with a 20-point value for Monday's index.

DJIA Index on Monday
Total price of all shares = $100
Total number of companies on the index = 5
Total price divided by number of companies = 20 points

Now we'll work with Tuesday's numbers to ensure that the index remains valued at 20 points. We'll do this by taking the total price of all the shares on the index that day and figuring out how to alter it so we are still left with 20 points. The calculation looks like this:

$90 ÷ ________ = 20 points.

We find that if we divide 90 by 4.5, we can obtain a value of 20. Therefore, 4.5 is our Dow divisor. Using the divisor allows us to report 20 points for the index on Tuesday—the same point value as Monday. Now, anyone following the index knows that its value hasn't changed. From this point forward, we will continue to translate the Dow's prices to points by using this divisor. When we do this, it accounts for Eggplant's stock split and ensures that the points reported aren't artificially low.

Now let me add a new wrinkle. What happens if, on Wednesday, the price of Durian stock falls to $2 a share due to an accounting scandal? In this case, we have company stock that has actually *dropped* in value and is worth *less*. For that reason, we would expect the cash value and the point value of the Dow to drop.

Wednesday

Stock	**Price**
Apple	$20
Banana	$20
Cantaloupe	$20
Durian	$ 2
Eggplant	$10
TOTAL	$72

Indeed, Durian's drop has affected the total price of the index by moving it from $90 on Tuesday down to $72 on Wednesday. We'll take that $72 figure and divide it by the Dow divisor. This keeps Eggplant's value intact but doesn't change Durian's influence.

$72/4.5 = 16 points

Now the points have dropped as well. That's because the value of the index actually *did* drop on Wednesday when Durian plummeted from $20 a share to $2.

If you thought that was fun (You thought it was fun, right? It's not just me?), then we'll kick things up a notch and try applying these ideas to the *real* Dow. (Data is not current, but reasonably close to actual numbers.)

Today's price of one share each of all 30 DJIA Stocks: $2,641.82

Today's divisor: 0.15571590501117 (You can find the current Dow Divisor on the home page of The Wall Street Journal. Check "Dow Averages Hour by Hour Performance and Volume")

That's a weird divisor, right? That divisor is the result of years of stock splits, mergers, takeovers, and other economic events. Every time something happens that could distort the value of the index, the divisor is adjusted to reflect that.

$2,641.82/0.15571590501117 = 16,965.64 points on the DJIA

Now we'll learn how a change in the share price of a stock affects the real-world index. Assume that the Dow was at 16,965.64 at the close of business yesterday. During today's trading session, 29 stocks on the index stayed exactly the same, while the price of a share of GE stock dropped $15. We are going to work with that $15 figure.

Take $1 and divide it by the divisor: 1/0.15571590501117 = 6.42

That means, for every $1 change in the price of the stocks, the points on the index change by 6.42. GE dropped by $15, so . . .

$15 X 6.42 = 96.3

Therefore, the Dow LOSES 96.3 points to close at 16,869.34.

Of course, it is highly unlikely that twenty-nine share prices will stay exactly the same while only one stock experiences a price change. All 30 stocks will fluctuate from one day to the next, and economic events (the stock splits we learned about, plus other activities) will continue to happen along the way. That's why the point system is so helpful. It gives us a stable number we can rely on—one that accounts for a drop in prices (one that affects value) as well as a *change* in prices (one that doesn't affect value).

At the time of this writing, the Dow has reported 21,987.56 points on the index. *The Wall Street Journal* (or just the *WSJ*) has published the current Dow divisor as 0.14523396877348. I can multiply 21,987.56 by 0.14523396877348 to come up with 3,193.34. That tells me the current total price of one share each of the 30 stocks on the index.

Here's a historical Dow chart from 1900 through today. Although there are a few steep drops, it's clear that the general trend for the index is up. Use this chart for reflection and study as you continue.

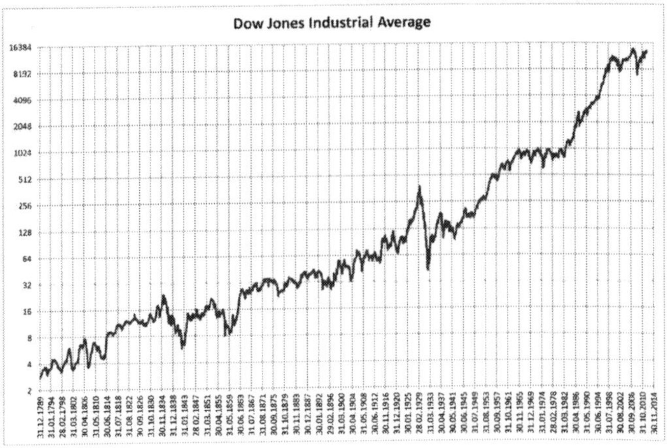

(Fig. 7.8)

Or, just for fun, see what kind of pictures you can make from the outline. Here's what I came up with:

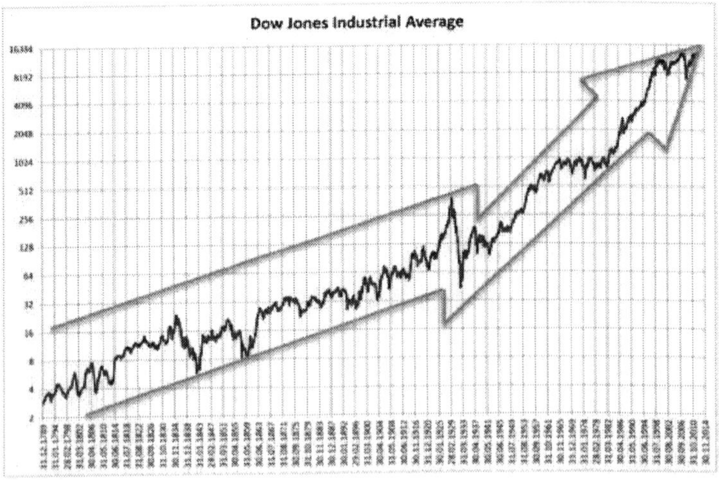

(Fig. 7.9)

The Dow chart reveals a distinct pattern with a message—not unlike a mysterious crop circle. "The sky's the limit!" it says.

Vocabulary

Blue chip stocks: The stock shares of large, well-established companies. Many blue chips are found on the DJIA.

DJIA: Dow Jones Industrial Average, a well-known stock index composed of thirty companies.

Dow divisor: A number used to preserve the value of the Dow Index. The divisor translates stock prices to points.

Index: A list of stocks.

Indices: The plural form of the word "index." Is too. Look it up.

Price-weighted index: A way of placing value on an index by basing it on the total cost of one share each of all of the stocks on the list.

Sector: An industry. Sectors of the economy are different industries where money is generated and spent, such as health care, energy, or utilities, for example.

Stock split: An economic event initiated by a company to simultaneously cut the price of existing stock shares while increasing the number of owned shares in the same proportion. For example, with a two-for-one stock split, the share price is cut in half, and existing shareholders have their stock shares doubled.

The S&P 500 Conundrum

To begin learning about the **S&P 500** index, we'll have to figure out what the odd code means. Start with the letters S and P. Anything come to mind?

"Shares and Prices" seems like a reasonable bet, but that's not it.

"Surging and Plunging" is a more dynamic take on the abbreviation, and certainly reflective of stock activity, but that's not it, either.

"**Scrilla and Paper**" would be a good modern name for the index, but sadly, I don't think this one is even being considered.

"S" & "P" stand for "Standard" and "Poor." When I first learned about these names, I just assumed that Standard and Poor were two rich old curmudgeons who started the index. I imagined them looking like **Statler and Waldorf** from *The Muppet Show*.

They totally look the part, right?

(Fig. 8.1)

Alas, there was no grandfatherly duo behind the S&P, at least not in the traditional sense. The index's beginnings trace all the way back to 1860, when financial analyst Henry Varnum Poor published the book *History of Railroads and Canals in the United States.* More than just light reading for a lazy Sunday afternoon, the book kept statistics on the financial operations of the major railroads. He updated it annually with his son Henry William.

In 1906, Luther Lee Blake founded the Standard Statistics Company, which tracked the movements of non-railroad companies. That company continued to publish its own index until it merged with Poor's in 1941 and became Standard and Poor's Corporation—S&P for short.

The S&P index is quite different from the Dow. It follows the stocks of a much larger cross-section of the market, and it includes small, medium, and large companies in its holdings. The number of stocks on the S&P positively dwarfs the Dow's little collection of 30. How many companies do you think are listed on the index? (Hint: it's called the S&P *500.*)

Actually, it's a trick question, because even though the S&P 500 lists 500 companies, a few of those companies offer different classes of their stock. Google (now known as Alphabet) offers class A shares (ticker symbol GOOGL) as well as class C shares (ticker symbol GOOG). Other companies that do this are Discover, Comcast, 21st Century Fox and News Corp. End result—there are 500 companies on the S&P, but they represent 505 stocks. Crazy, right? This little factoid could work as an awesome icebreaker on a first date. This guy is killing it.

Gal: Really? 505? No fair! You tricked me!
Guy: Heh, heh. I've got a million of 'em.
Let's have another drink and I'll tell you more about indices.
(Fig. 8.2)

OK, put romance aside for a moment (always a problem in a discussion about stocks) and focus on the S&P. Here's a look at the different sectors that can be found on the list.

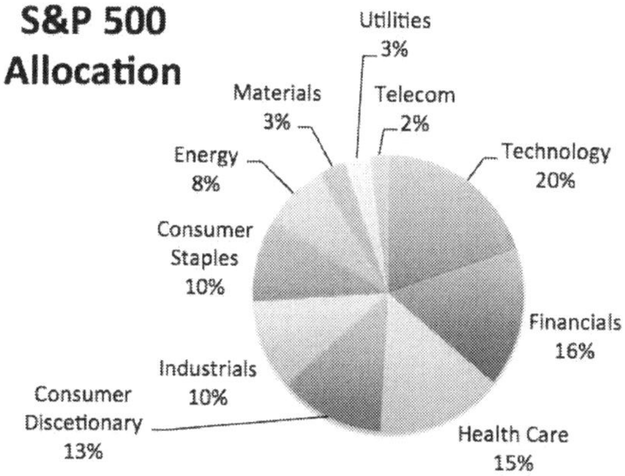

(Fig. 8.3)

Here are some of the companies in each sector:

Technology: Apple, Facebook, Microsoft
Financials: Bank of America, Citigroup, Goldman Sachs Group
Health Care: Bristol-Meyers Squib, CIGNA Corp., Pfizer, Inc.
Consumer Discretionary: Advance Auto Parts, Best Buy, Home Depot, Inc.
Industrials: Caterpillar, Inc., General Electric, United Parcel Service
Consumer Staples: Campbell Soup, CVS Health, General Mills
Energy: Chevron, Phillips 66, Halliburton Co.
Materials: Monsanto Co., Sherwin-Williams, DowDuPont
Utilities: American Electric Power, PPL Corp., Edison International
Telecom: Verizon Communications, AT&T Inc., Century Link Inc.

(You may have noticed that some of the stocks on this list are also on the Dow. That's not a problem. Remember that an index is just a way to study the market by focusing on representative stocks. Some stocks are so important to the economy that they will show up on multiple indices.)

Together these 505 stocks account for around 80% of the economy. For that reason, the S&P 500 is considered to be the index that best reflects general market conditions in the United States. The Dow, while it contains extremely large and profitable companies, is a little too restricted with its 30 stocks to serve as a general indicator. (Though you wouldn't necessarily come to that conclusion from watching the news. The Dow is an institution in the stock market world, and for that reason, it will always be regarded as a weather vane for the economy.)

One phenomenon that illustrates the importance of the S&P is the **S&P effect**. Whenever the S&P announces that there will be an addition to its list, the newly- selected company typically experiences a 7% rise in its stock price. (Williams, 2016)

But does the S&P effect last? Eh…not so much. Word on the street is that it's just hype that eventually dies down.

The S&P index has a different system of valuation from the Dow. It takes the price of a share of stock and multiplies it by the number of shares outstanding to come up with a number called the **market cap**, short for **market capitalization**. The market caps of all the stocks are then added together to get a total dollar value. This makes the S&P a **market cap-weighted index**. Here's a simplified example of how it works:

S&P

Stock	Price	Shares Outstanding	Total
Stock A	$50	100	$5,000
Stock B	$60	75	$4,500
Stock C	$40	50	$2,000
Total Market Cap			$11,500

You'll notice that a stock with a high share price doesn't necessarily have the highest market cap. Stock B is the highest-priced stock at $60, but with only 75 shares outstanding, its market cap is smaller than the lower-priced Stock A.[1]

I'm sure you've heard references to "mid cap" and "large cap" stocks before. Now you know that the "cap" being referred to is a value for the company based on the market cap formula. Here's how the cap sizes are determined:

Small cap = less than $2 billion in market capitalization
(Fossil, Frontier Communications, Diamond Offshore Drilling)

Mid cap = between $2 billion and $10 billion in market capitalization
(Chipotle, The Gap, Seagate Technology)

Large cap = between $10 billion and $100 billion in market capitalization
(Pepsi, Intel, Disney)

Mega cap = $200 billion and up in market capitalization
(Apple, Exxon, Microsoft)

Back in 1957, the market caps of all the S&P 500 companies on the list totaled 172 billion. By 1980, that number had jumped to 925 billion. Fast forward to today where the largest company on the list, Apple, is worth 815 billion just on its own. If you add in that amount, along with the market caps for the other 499 stocks on the index, what value would you place on the current total S&P market cap? Any guesses?

If you said, "Somewhere in the trillions," I'll accept it. Frankly, I start losing touch with what numbers even mean by the time I get to the billions. But the actual number, thanks to a rallying stock market that has been churning since the beginning of 2017, is now at $20 trillion.

The S&P doesn't use its market cap for reporting, though. Just like the Dow (and other indices, for that matter) it uses a divisor to translate the dollar value to points. So not only does the S&P divisor account for the economic events that could misrepresent the index's value, it also reduces those trillions of dollars to a number that can actually register in people's brains. In recent times, the divisor has been around 8,900,000,000 or so. That's good—we need a big number to break down that massive market cap figure. Here's how it works out:

20,000,000,000,000/8,900,000,000 = 2,448 points on the S&P Index

The top five stocks on the S&P index in terms of market cap are Apple, Amazon, Alphabet GOOGL, Microsoft, and Facebook. We can figure out what percentage of the index they occupy by taking a company's market cap and dividing it by the 20 trillion total of the index. For Apple, it looks like this:

815,000,000,000/20,000,000,000,000 = 0.04075.

In other words, Apple stock accounts for about 4% of the entire index. I won't give you the percentages for the other stocks in that group because I know you probably want to look up the numbers and do the math yourself. (Gold star for you!) But I'll say this—together that group makes up more than 10% of the total S&P value.

With the market cap system, larger companies can exert more influence over the index when they experience a price change. In the event that Apple suffers a stunning downturn, its stock might lose 20% of its value. Here's how that would affect the S&P:

0.04075 (Apple's percentage of the index) X .20 (the amount of loss) = 0.00815 or a .815% drop in the S&P.

A .815% loss may not seem like much at first glance, but remember, with a total market cap of $20 trillion, that tiny percentage amounts to $163 billion. And in the event that the 20% downturn is something internet-related that affects *all* of those top five stocks, the numbers are even more shocking:

.10 (combined percentage of the top five S&P stocks) x .20 (the amount of loss) = 0.02, or a 2% drop.

That 2% amounts to two trillion dollars—the entire GDP of France![2]

By comparison, the price movements of small cap companies are little more than a microscopic blip on the index. The movements of all of the small cap companies *combined* (even major movements) would probably not match the movement of one large cap stock. That's important information if you want to understand the nuances of the S&P.

Here's a historical S&P chart showing the movements of the S&P from 1950 through 2016. Examine it with due diligence, or just skip ahead to my Rorschach-like interpretation.

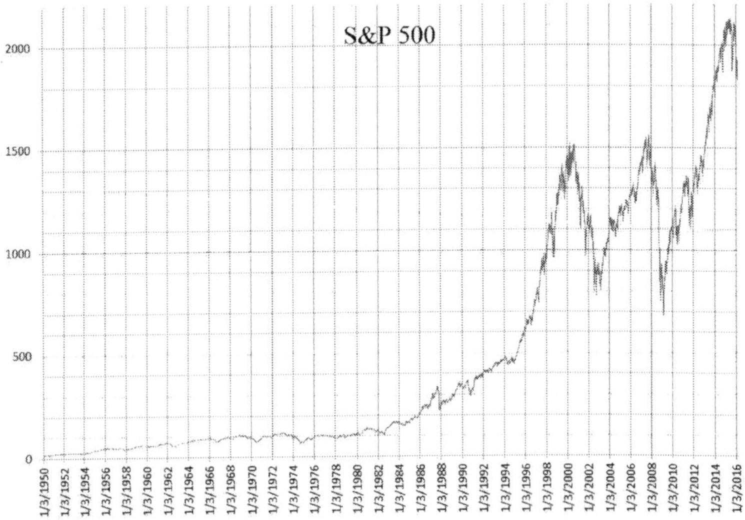

(Fig. 8.4)

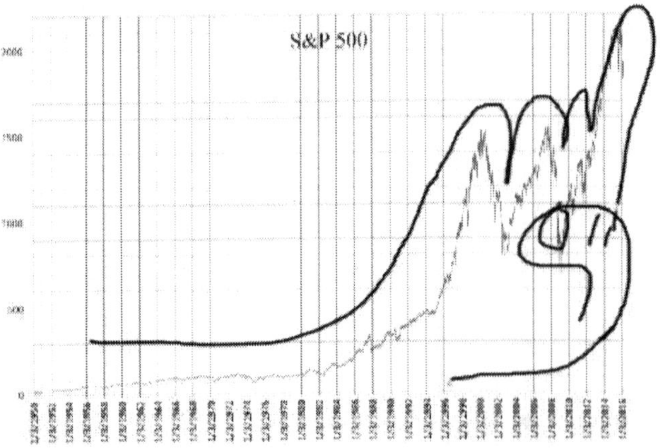

(Fig. 8.5)

Yet again, the chart reveals a secret message. "You'll be number one!" it says, enticing you to invest. It also suggests a total market collapse around 2020. But tomorrow be damned! Live for today!

[1]Many people argue that a market cap-weighted index is superior to the Dow's price-weighted system, and this is a perfect example of their reasoning. Stock B has more of an influence over the index because it generates more money, regardless of its share price. I have to say, this does seem like the most logical way to assign value.

The Dow, on the other hand, uses the share price and the Dow divisor to determine the number of "points" a company is worth. That means that General Electric, with a small share price of $25.14 but a whopping $271.49 billion market cap, only accounts for 173.1 points on the index. Goldman Sachs has a significantly smaller market cap of $87 billion, and yet it commands 1,555.28 points on the Dow because of its hefty $255.88 share price. If you hear people saying that the Dow isn't a good measure of the stock market, this is why. It simply looks at individual share prices without taking into account how many of those shares have been purchased.

[2]This is why many folks feel uncomfortable with the tech industry commanding such a large portion of our economy. In the event that our efforts in this sector are surpassed or rendered obsolete, the effects will be devastating and far reaching.

Vocabulary

Market cap: Short for "market capitalization," which is a way to value a company. A market cap is found by taking the price of one share of stock and multiplying it by the number of shares outstanding.

Market cap-weighted index: An index that determines value by totaling the market cap of every company on the list. The total market cap dollar value is then translated to points using a divisor.

S&P 500: Standard and Poor's. The abbreviation for a stock index that includes over 500 U.S. companies that are important to the economy (both domestically and worldwide).

S&P Effect: A temporary surge in stock price when a company is about to be admitted to the S&P index.

Scrilla and Paper: Slang for money

Statler and Waldorf: The two grumpy old Muppets that sat in the box seats on the Muppet Show, constantly complaining about the quality of entertainment and heckling the acts. Some FTW quotes:

> *Waldorf: Well, the opening was catchy.*
> *Statler: So is smallpox.*
>
> *(After Debbie Harry sings "One Way or Another")*
> *Waldorf: I wonder who she was looking for.*
> *Statler: Probably the guy that booked her on this crummy show!*
>
> *Waldorf: Shakespeare would have hated that.*
> *Statler: You should know. You dated his sister.*
> *Waldorf: Boy, was she ugly.*

Got Nasdaq?

The last of the "Big Three" stock indices is the ***Nasdaq Composite***, also commonly referred to as "**the Nasdaq**." This can be a little confusing, because the **NASDAQ** is also the name of a stock exchange, where stocks are bought and sold.

You can make an effort to keep those two entities separate in your head—one is an exchange and one is an index—but it may not matter that much, since they are almost inextricably connected. The Nasdaq Composite Index includes *every single stock* listed on the NASDAQ Exchange. So if you're following the movement of "the Nasdaq," the distinction may not be that important. Whether it's the exchange or the index, you're still talking about the same group of stocks.

Now that you have this information, what can you infer about the Nasdaq Composite?

- There are over 3,000 companies included on the Nasdaq Composite Index (because there are over 3,000 companies listed on the NASDAQ Exchange).
- The Nasdaq Composite is mainly comprised of tech stocks because the NASDAQ Exchange is mainly comprised of tech stocks.
- When you hear reports about how the Nasdaq is doing, you are essentially hearing how the tech sector is doing, not how the general market is doing.

Why follow an index that only tracks this sector? As mentioned previously, tech stocks are responsible for a huge chunk of the economy. And due to their speculative nature, they're also volatile. When they hold headline-making IPOs or experience panicked sell-outs, it influences the purchase and sale of stocks worldwide and determines the level of investor confidence in the markets. Even if you aren't directly invested in any tech stocks, you need to be aware of what they are doing. The effect of their movements—in either direction—will eventually trickle down to all of us.

As for how the Nasdaq Composite Index is calculated, this is directly from the Nasdaq website:

The NASDAQ Composite Index is a market capitalization-weighted index. The value of the Index equals the aggregate value of the Index share weights, also known as the Index Shares, of each of the Index Securities multiplied by each such security's last sale price, and divided by the divisor of the index. The divisor serves the purpose of scaling such aggregate value to a lower order of magnitude which is more desirable for reporting purposes. (NASDAQ composite index methodology, n.d.)

If you're feeling a bit dizzy after reading that and considering throwing in the towel—don't. That is what "The Man" wants you to do, so all of the great stock market opportunities are left to him and his cronies.

The Man

The Man is the head of "the establishment" **put in** place to "bring us down." Though nobody has physically seen "**the man**," he is assumed to be a male **caucasian** between the ages of 25-40 and is rumored to have a substantial amount of acquired wealth, presumably acquired by exploiting those whom his "establishment" is "keeping down."

*"**Damn The Man**!" -Victim of the "**establishment**"*

(Fig. 9.1)

While that index description may have sounded like a lot of stock market mumbo-jumbo, you actually already know exactly what it means. Behold the original content and the Market Mojo translation:

The NASDAQ Composite Index is a market capitalization-weighted index.

No problem. We know what market cap-weighted means. It's valued just like the S&P 500.

The value of the Index equals the aggregate value of the Index share weights, also known as the Index Shares, of each of the Index Securities multiplied by each such security's last sale price, and divided by the divisor of the index.

Whoop-de-doo. This is nothing more than a description of how market caps are calculated. You could also just say, "Stock price for each company times the number of shares outstanding. Add those numbers up and then divide by the divisor."

The divisor serves the purpose of scaling such aggregate value to a lower order of magnitude which is more desirable for reporting purposes.

Yeah, yeah. We know what a divisor is—it changes dollars to points and makes the day-to-day reading of the index easier to follow. In the case of the S&P, it gets us out of the "trillions" range and gives us a number that is easier to understand. "More desirable for reporting purposes," indeed. This isn't nearly as hard as they make it out to be. Are you feeling empowered now?

There's not much left to do except look at the historical chart and my insightful interpretation. If I do say so, I think it's my best work yet.

(Fig. 9.2)

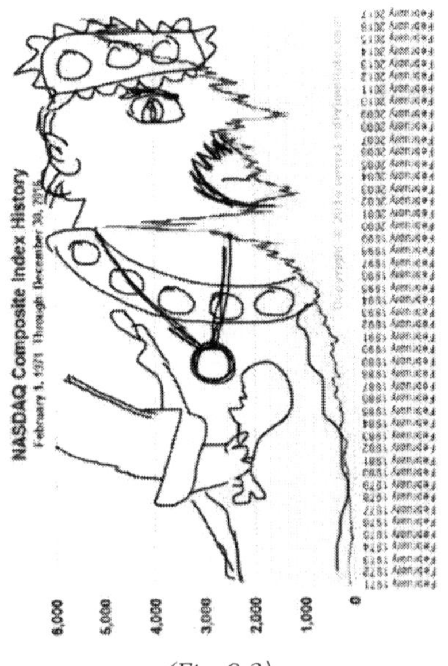

(Fig. 9.3)

I know it doesn't have anything to do with investing, but look! I made Henry VIII!

Here's a quick review so we can put this new information into perspective and see how it fits in with the other things we've learned.

There are two stock exchanges in the United States: The NASDAQ and the NYSE. These are basically just stores that sell individual stocks.

There are three main stock indices, or lists of stocks.

The Dow Jones Index (DJIA): An index of 30 blue chip American stocks. Most of these are sold on the NYSE, with a few sold on the NASDAQ. Although often quoted and discussed in stock circles, the Dow is not the best indicator of market conditions for two reasons. 1) Its list of 30 stocks is too small to illustrate a true cross-section of the market. 2) It uses a price-weighted system of valuation, which gives weight to the stocks with the biggest share prices (regardless of how many of those shares have been sold).

The S&P 500: A collection of 505 stocks from different sectors representing small cap, mid cap, and large cap companies. These stocks are sold on the NYSE and the NASDAQ. The S&P is generally considered to be the best indicator of general market conditions because of its diverse holdings and its market-cap weighted system of valuation.

The Nasdaq Composite Index: A market cap-weighted index containing over 4,000 stocks that are only sold on the NASDAQ exchange. The Nasdaq is a tech-heavy collection of stocks, so its reports are a reflection of the current state of the tech sector. The Nasdaq is an important index to follow because tech companies are responsible for a large component of the economy.

You may be wondering, "What then, is the link between these stock exchanges and *me*? How exactly do I get my money out there into the market to start buying stocks?

Perhaps you remember an episode from *Friends*, when Monica decided it was time for her to invest:

> Rachel: But Monica, you don't know the first thing about the stock market.
>
> Monica: What's to know? Buy low, sell high! Bears! Bulls! (Picks up phone) Yes. Manhattan. Telephone number for the stock . . . selling store.

That's funny 'cause it's true. Read on to make sure that you know how to contact the stock-selling store so you can purchase your own shares.

You Give Me Fever

Readers, have you noticed any of the following? Elevated temperature, chills, loss of appetite, fatigue, aches or pains? Don't be alarmed, I have the symptoms, too. It's an epidemic. We've got . . . **INVESTING FEVER!!!**[1]

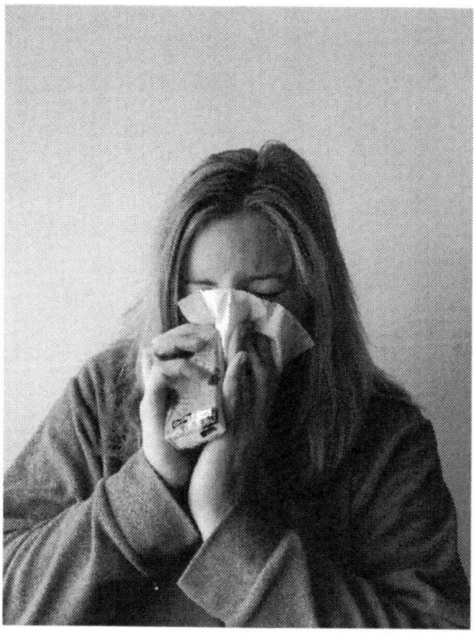

This woman doesn't need medication, she needs ten shares of Amazon, stat!
(Fig. 10.1)

OK, that might be a bit too corny, even for me. But gosh darn it, I think it's exciting. You should too, because this is the part where you learn how to take action and become a real, honest-to-goodness investor.

To purchase most stocks, you need to use a middleman, or a **stockbroker**. It's pretty much the same concept as visiting a restaurant. You don't just march back into the kitchen and ask the chef a bunch of questions about food and prices and place your order right there, do you? Of course not. You wait for a waiter to bring you a menu. Then you see what the offerings are, check the prices, and make your decision. The waiter takes your order back to the kitchen, where he is responsible for making sure that it gets recorded and delivered.

Brokers work the same way, serving as the link between you and the company from which you are purchasing stock. (And just like restaurant waiters, brokers will expect a tip for their services.) You have two options for brokers:

Full-Service Broker: This is a finance expert who is assigned to you and your account. She will answer questions, provide advice, and make stock sales and purchases on your behalf. If you are apprehensive about investing on your own and would feel better with personalized assistance, this could be the way to go.

Full-service brokers can also do more than just manage your stock investments. You may rely on them to manage your retirement funds, give you tax advice, and even help you figure out a college savings plan for Junior. There's no denying that there is a "one-stop-shopping" appeal to this kind of arrangement. Having a full-service broker relieves you of doing any of the heavy-duty research on your own. You just explain your needs and financial goals, and the broker will handle the rest.

This kind of convenience won't be cheap, though. Most full-service brokers charge an annual fee that is equal to a percentage of the total amount of funds they manage for you. So if your broker manages your $150,000 portfolio and her fee is an annual 2% of that, she's getting $3,000 of your yearly take. That really adds up over time. (She'll also get that same percentage if your fund *loses* money, which might be a bitter pill to swallow.)

Another problem with traditional, full-service brokers is that they have been able to operate in a fairly opaque manner for some time now. Until the **Dodd-Frank Act** of 2010, many brokers encouraged their clients to buy particular stocks or funds not because the products were in the client's best interests, but because they were getting kickbacks from those stocks and funds. Even worse, the brokers' payments were often funneled to them circuitously so that it wasn't immediately clear from the financial reports that the selected funds were giving the brokers compensation. Although these arrangements are euphemistically referred to as "commissions," I take issue with that term. At any rate, the Dodd-Frank Act now requires brokers to disclose any and all of these "commissions" to potential buyers. The catch, though, is that the provision only applies to retirement accounts such as 401(k)s—not other kinds of investment funds. So be sure to ask lots of questions about how the fees are structured when you are talking to a potential broker. There's nothing wrong with flat-out asking, "Are you recommending this stock because you have a financial relationship with the company?" Look 'em dead in the eye while you do it.

I don't mean to suggest that every full-service broker or financial advisor is out to scam you. There are *lots* of reputable advisors out there. If you find one that you think is worth the expense, there's nothing wrong with that. I *do* recommend that you increase your chances of finding someone trustworthy and reliable by only considering those with professional credentials such as a CFP®(Certified Financial Planner) or a CPA® (Certified Public Accountant).

Discount Broker: A discount broker isn't just one person; it's an online brokerage firm made up of many financial advisors and company representatives. This is a good way to go if you are more of a DIY investor. By opening an account with a discount brokerage, you can buy and sell stocks on your own—no assistance needed.

There are a number of reputable discount brokerages online, and most of them offer surprisingly good educational tools such as glossaries, informative videos, and even entire courses. You can also give them a call and talk to a representative who can give you more information about the services they offer. Keep in mind, these representatives aren't a substitute for a personal broker—they are there to get you to sign up for an account with their company.

The fee structure for discount brokerages varies, but they usually make their money by charging clients for every trade they make. These fees can add up to large sums over time but are still probably only a fraction of what you would pay to a full service broker.

Here are some general questions to keep in mind as you shop around for a discount broker:

- Does the company require a minimum deposit before clients can invest? (Try to find one with no minimum. They are out there.)
- How much does the firm charge per trade? (Don't necessarily look for the cheapest trades out there, but consider this cost along with other information. If the trading fees are ridiculously low, the firm is making its money in some other area, trust me.)
- What are the other fees that are associated with this firm? (Are they going to charge you a fee just to transfer in funds from your bank? Do they have maintenance fees and/or monthly fees?)
- Is there a help desk or support of any kind? Are there fees for using these services?

The advent of online brokerages is a fantastic development. We've always needed another investing option that allows us to bypass the expensive personal stockbrokers and take a more active role in managing our finances. If you don't find this kind of access exciting, you may not remember the good ol' days when the stock market was largely a wealthy insiders' club. Do you remember the old **E.F. Hutton** commercials? I sure do—they perfectly exemplified the exclusivity that was so common in the markets back then. Only a few people had access to market information, and others were left just trying to listen in.

Compare that to now, a time when anyone can get in the game. It's high time that this market access became freely available to everyone.

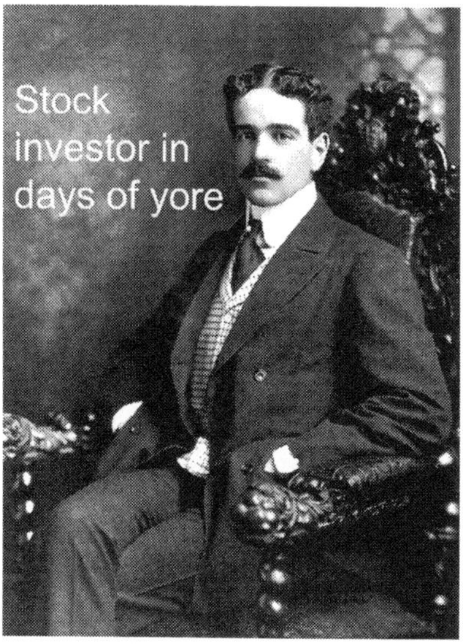

If you weren't a rich white guy, your stock options were limited, to say the least.
(Fig. 10.2)

This gal just bought ten shares of Coca-Cola at a stop light! How cool is that? (OK, not so cool since she's texting and driving. Don't do that. That's dangerous. Always pull the car over and come to a complete stop before engaging in market transactions.)
(Fig. 10.3)

I say, POWER TO THE PEOPLE!

I'm glad we're ending on a high note, because now you can take that energy and confidence and channel it into your next quiz. You're gonna do *great*.

[1]If you have something that looks like this, it is *not* investing fever. It is definitely **tick fever**. Do not call your broker. Go see a doctor right away.

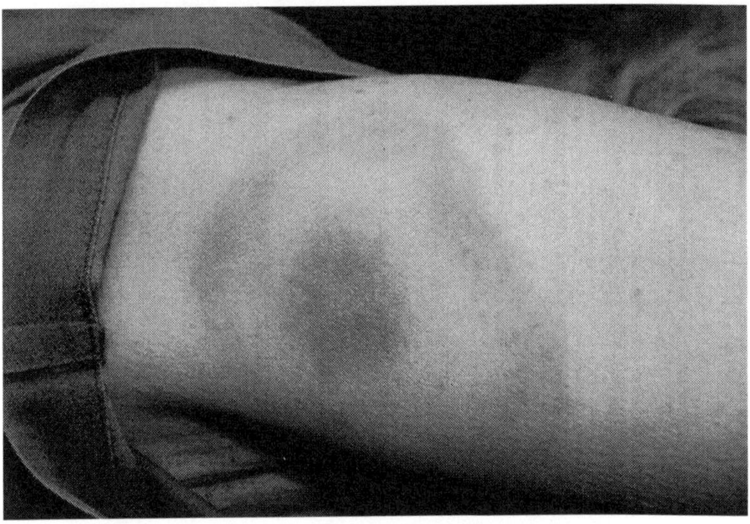

(Fig. 10.4)

Vocabulary

Discount broker: A brokerage firm that serves as the link between you and the market. As a client of the firm, you can buy and sell stocks on your own behalf.

Dodd-Frank Act: A huge piece of legislation passed in 2010 during the Obama administration as a reaction to the 2008 financial crisis. United States Senator Christopher Dodd and United States Representative Barney Frank sponsored the bill, which introduced stricter regulations on banks, insurance companies, and credit agencies. The new law aimed to put an end to the speculative trading and poor lending practices that led to a worldwide financial downfall. The act also included special provisions to protect consumers from predatory financial advisors who steered clients into buying products and services that were not in their best interests.

E.F. Hutton: A brokerage firm founded by Edward Francis Hutton. The firm had very popular commercials in the 1970s and 1980s that all had the same format: Someone is making polite conversation at a party, and casually mentions that she is a client of the firm by saying, "Well my broker is E.F. Hutton, and E.F. Hutton says . . ." At this point, the party stops, dishes drop, and a hush comes over the crowd. Everyone leans in as close as possible to find out what the hot stock tips are. I don't know . . . it was funny back then.

Full-service broker: A financial professional who is working just for you. The broker devises an investing plan that matches your particular investing goals. He or she may also work with you on a variety of other investment plans such as retirement or college savings.

Investing fever: Sometimes confused with the flu or hot flashes, a feeling of excitement and anxiety mixed with a desire to increase one's wealth through the immediate purchase of stock shares.

Stockbroker: The middleman between you and the market. A broker makes purchases on your behalf.

Tick fever: An illness resulting from the bite of a tick. Different kinds of tick bites are common in different regions. In general though, symptoms include headache, fatigue, and muscle aches. With Lyme disease, you may also experience joint pain.

QUIZ 2

1. What are the three main stock indices?
    a. DJIA, NASDAQ, S&P 400
    b. Wall Street, DJIA, dominatrices
    c. NASDAQ, S&P 300, DJIA
    d. S&P 500, NASDAQ, DJIA

2. Who published the first stock index?
    a. Charles Darwin
    b. Charles Dow
    c. Charles Nelson Reilly
    d. Beyonce, writing as "Sasha Fierce"

3. The original Dow list was mainly comprised of companies in what industry?
    a. Railroads
    b. Plastics
    c. Energy
    d. Tech

4. Which company is listed in the Dow Jones Industrial Average?
    a. Apple
    b. McHooty's
    c. Exxon
    d. Amazon

5. Which sentence best describes the Dow divisor?
    a. A number that converts stock shares to dividends
    b. A number that converts stock prices to stock points
    c. A number that converts stock prices to percentages
    d. A number that converts stock shares to points

6. Which number is most likely to be a Dow divisor?
    a. 0.145687320
    b. 4
    c. 647 billion
    d. 8.9 billion

7. Which paper publishes the Dow divisor daily?
    a. *GRIT*
    b. *CNN Money*
    c. *The WSJ*
    d. *Stock Market Time*

8. How many stocks are listed on the S&P 500?
    a. 499
    b. 5000
    c. 500
    d. 505

9. How do you calculate the market cap for a company?
    a. Price of one share of stock times number of shareholders
    b. Price of one share of stock times 100
    c. Price of one share of stock times the Dow divisor
    d. Price of one share of stock times total shares outstanding

10. Which of these is most likely an S&P divisor?
    a. 647 billion
    b. 8.9 billion

c. 0.145687320
d. 4

11. One difference between a full-service broker and a discount broker is:
    a. The full-service broker is cheaper
    b. The full-service broker isn't accessible online
    c. A discount broker is usually cheaper
    d. A discount broker gives personalized investing advice

12. All stock indices report their numbers by taking an average of the share price of each stock on the list.
    a. True
    b. False

13. Which of the following is a professional credential?
    a. CSA: Certified Stock Analyst
    b. CSB: Certified Stock Broker
    c. CFA: Certified Financial Advisor
    d. CFP: Certified Financial Planner

14. What is the benefit of checking a stock index daily?
    a. It allows you to see how the entire stock market is doing at a glance.
    b. It tells you if a particular stock has fallen or risen in value.
    c. It allows you to see how a particular cross-section of stocks is doing at a glance.
    d. It makes you look cool to be thoughtfully reading the finance section of the newspaper.

15. The Dow is a market cap-weighted index.
    a. True
    b. False

Answer Key for Quiz 2

1. D

   Just for the record, "Wall Street" is never a real answer on these quizzes.

2. B

   I'm really not concerned if you don't know who Charles Darwin is, but if you've never heard of Charles Nelson Reilly, you go Google that amazingly talented man *right now.*

3. A

   Although later, there were so many railroads that they split off into their own index.

4. C

   It's easy to think that the answer is Apple at first glance, just because it's so well-known and profitable. But remember—DJIA stocks are usually older companies.

5. B

   Points are what we read about in the news, but they're based on prices.

6. A

   You obviously don't need to commit this to memory, but it's good to know the ballpark figure.

7. C

   Is *GRIT* still published?

8. D

   This one is a great icebreaker at parties or functions, remember?

9. D

   The share price times the number of shares outstanding gives you an idea of the company's value.

10. B

    It's unlikely that this will come up again in your studies, but it's good to know that the giant divisor is needed because the value of the S&P index is so massive.

11. C

    Although there are no guarantees, online brokers are usually the cheapest option for an investor.

12. B

    We wouldn't have done all of that computing in the last few chapters if the indices just take a mean average.

13. D

    A Certified Financial Planner is a widely-accepted professional credential.

14. C

    You may have jumped the gun by choosing "A," but remember, the indices don't report on the *entire* market—just the companies that are listed with them.

15. B

    But I made you stop and think, didn't I?

If you successfully completed this quiz, then you are already familiar with market-related terms that you see online and in print. That will certainly kick up your Mojo another notch. Enjoy the surge of power as you continue to Part Three.

Part 3

Taking Stock of the Situation

The Hare and the Hedgehog: A New Interpretation of a Classic
A Game Called Risk
"Denial" Is a River in Egypt, but "Diversification" Is a Lake in Papua New Guinea
I'm Gonna Pop Some Stocks, Got Twenty Dollars in My Pocket

Taking Stock of the Situation

By this point, you've realized that the stock market is not the mystical cabal that it is made out to be. Maybe you're even starting to consider investing some of your own money—that's great. Now that you are warming up to the idea, this is a good time to do a little self-reflection and think about investing strategies that are a good match for your financial situation and your personality. Establishing this investor profile is the springboard you'll use to launch yourself into the market space.

Remember—there are countless books, websites, and videos out there that insist there is some big secret to investing. Many of them propagate the myth that the "professionals" are sitting behind closed doors, using their special decoder rings and snickering to themselves because they know the *real* way to beat the market. I call BS. The right way to invest is the way that's right for *you* and no one else. By getting to know yourself a little better and indulging in some real financial reflection, you'll be prepared to make decisions that are in your best interests, and you'll be less likely to fall for silly sales pitches that promise impossible results.

On that note, it's time to start this journey of self-discovery.

The Hare and The Hedgehog: A New Interpretation of a Classic Fable[1]

What is the difference between the following two sentences?

I invest in the market.
I trade in the market.

I wouldn't be surprised if you think they mean the same thing, even though the sentences use two different words to describe activities in the stock market. While "investing" and "trading" are terms that you will hear all the time, you may not know that these words refer to two distinctly different approaches to making money. You need to know if you are an investor or a trader before you can accurately describe your market philosophy.

Informative pamphlet I am working on.
When did they go out of fashion, anyway? Are there any **pamphleteers** *left?*
(Fig. 11.1)

Investors take a slow and steady approach to the market, and they put their money into businesses that they understand and believe in. They aren't influenced by rumors or hype surrounding the "next big thing," and they aren't out looking for hot stock tips. Investors are looking for companies that are stable and have long-term prospects. I'm talking about holding on to company stock for a ten-year minimum, and usually longer than that. In this fable, the investors are hedgehogs.

Typical hedgehog on a leisurely, low-stress investing journey.
(Fig. 11.2)

Investors accept the fact that the market is going to have ups and downs. Their strategy to deal with this is to ride it out because they know that in the long run, the numbers will work in their favor and that they will eventually wind up with more money than they started with. They play the long game.

I'm inclined to agree with the investors on this point. If you think back to the historical index charts from Part Two, you'll recall that apart from a few clunker periods, the markets always trend up. *Way* up, if you compare the beginning to the present.

Now granted, when you scale things from 1900 until today, it really paves over the bad years and gives the illusion of a mostly smooth ride to the top. If you want to get a better idea of what the real ups and downs are and figure out if you are a true hedgehog or not, then look at this list that shows the DJIA annual returns year by year. Careful—there are some real doozies on there!

Dow Jones Industrial Average: Annual Returns					
Year	**Percent**	**Year**	**Percent**	**Year**	**Percent**
1901	-8.7	1939	-3.9	1977	-17.3
1902	-0.4	1940	-12.7	1978	-3.1
1903	-23.6	1941	-15.3	1979	4.2
1904	41.7	1942	7.6	1980	14.9
1905	38.2	1943	13.8	1981	-9.2
1906	-1.9	1944	12.1	1982	19.6
1907	-37.7	1945	26.7	1983	20.3
1908	46.6	1946	-8.1	1984	-3.7
1909	15.0	1947	2.2	1985	27.7
1910	-17.9	1948	-2.1	1986	22.6
1911	0.4	1949	13.1	1987	2.3
1912	7.6	1950	17.4	1988	11.8
1913	-10.3	1951	14.4	1989	27.0
1914	-30.7	1952	8.4	1990	-4.3
1915	81.7	1953	-3.8	1991	20.3
1916	-4.2	1954	44.0	1992	4.2
1917	-21.7	1955	20.8	1993	13.7
1918	10.5	1956	2.3	1994	2.1
1919	30.5	1957	-12.8	1995	33.5
1920	-32.9	1958	34.0	1996	26.0
1921	12.7	1959	16.4	1997	22.6
1922	21.7	1960	-9.3	1998	16.1
1923	-3.3	1961	18.7	1999	25.2

1924	26.2	1962	-10.8	2000	-6.2
1925	30.0	1963	17.0	2001	-7.1
1926	0.3	1964	14.6	2002	-16.8
1927	28.8	1965	10.9	2003	25.3
1928	48.2	1966	-18.9	2004	3.1
1929	-17.2	1967	15.2	2005	-0.6
1930	-33.8	1968	4.3	2006	16.3
1931	-52.7	1969	-15.2	2007	6.4
1932	-23.1	1970	4.8	2008	-33.8
1933	66.8	1971	6.1	2009	18.8
1934	4.1	1972	14.6	2010	11.0
1935	38.6	1973	-16.6	2011	5.5
1936	24.8	1974	-27.6	2012	7.3
1937	-32.8	1975	38.3	2013	26.5
1938	28.0	1976	17.9	2014	7.5

How secure in your investments would you have been in, say, 1931, 1974, or 2008?

As an investor, you have to be prepared to stand your ground and hang on to your stock shares, even when their prices are plummeting. You have committed to this project for the long haul, which means you are going to sit back and let share appreciation, dividends, and time work their magic. You are going to base your success on the returns you get per year, or perhaps even per *decade*. Because of this hands-off approach, this is sometimes called the "**buy and hold**" method or the "**set and forget**" method.

Traders, on the other hand, look at those same charts and say, "To hell with riding the wave! I just want to buy cheap stocks, wait for the prices to climb, and then sell all of my shares at a huge profit before the market takes a nose dive." Traders are the hares of the fable.

Hares hop along the investing journey.
(Fig. 11.3)

I'll have to agree with the traders on that point, too. Who in their right mind would argue with "Buy low, sell high?" Also, I'm a bit jealous of the traders' complete hedonism. When it comes to investing, I just quietly assume that I'm a slave to the market and have to tolerate the ups with the downs, but not these guys. They're always on the prowl for their next big ka-ching moment, and refuse to believe that they have to take any hits along the way.

Traders rarely have much of an interest in any company they invest in—they pick stocks based on how they're going to do in the short term, not the long term. And given that stock market fortunes can change quickly, traders stay busy. Some of them are buying and selling every few minutes. That's because traders tend to measure their success based on their returns per day. This method is the complete opposite of "set and forget." It's more like "**turn and burn**."

Another interesting note about the difference between investors and traders is how they interpret market news. Investors want the market to move *up*. They know that they are holding on to their shares no matter what, so obviously, when prices increase, the value of their investment goes up.

Traders, on the other hand, don't care *which* direction the market is moving in as long as it is moving. Because they approach investing like a game, they can find ways to make earnings when the market is up or down. They can buy *or* sell, because they are either getting cheap deals or making quick profits.

How do you know which one of these is the best approach? Easy—just think back to the moral of the original, universal tale. "Fast and flashy" doesn't win the race, "slow and steady" does. While the investing path isn't a *Wolf of Wall Street* thrill ride, it's dependable. Believe me, dependability is a quality that you will come to love when it comes to long-term growth and earnings. So consider investing the majority of your available money. Although it exposes you to a moderate amount of risk, you will almost certainly realize positive growth over time.

Do you have a trading itch that you need to scratch? Go ahead and indulge, I suppose, but I strongly encourage you to limit the amount of money you spend placing those bets (and honestly, trading is pretty much the same thing as betting). If you only trade with an amount of money that you can stand to lose, then you won't be in dire straits when you eventually roll snake eyes.

[1]The original Grimm's fairy tale was "**Der Hase** und **der Igel**," translated from German as "The Hare and the Hedgehog" before it later became known as "The Tortoise and The Hare" in English-language texts. However, I see no reason to deviate from source material. Plus, hedgehogs are adorable.

Vocabulary

Buy and hold: The practice of holding on to investments for long periods of time in order to attain the highest possible value. Using this method means the investor will go through some periods of losses and uneven earnings, but will most likely realize an overall profit at the end of the investing period.

der Hase: German for *the hare*

der Igel: German for *the hedgehog*

Investor: Someone who purchases investments to hold on to for the long term.

Pamphleteer: Someone who writes and distributes pamphlets, usually in order to support an idea or belief, or possibly to criticize an idea or a belief. A pamphleteer usually writes about topics that are political in nature.

Set and forget: Same as "buy and hold."

Trader: Someone who buys and sells frequently in order to get the highest returns possible and to avoid losses.

Turn and burn: Not a real investing term, just something I made up to characterize the practice of buying and selling securities quickly in order make profits and avoid losses. "Set and forget" is a pretty snappy slogan, so I felt like I needed one for traders to maintain balance. Maybe it will catch on.

A Game Called Risk

There are two terms I'm going to introduce to you that are absolutely critical to your financial education. If you ever plan to talk to a financial advisor, I really want you to have these terms nailed down before you walk in the door. They are the basis for all of your financial decisions.

Risk Capacity = How much money you can lose without going into debt
Risk Tolerance = How much money you can lose without losing sleep over it

Here's an easy, two-question quiz you can take to figure out your risk capacity.

Question 1:
Do you struggle to make ends meet every month?

- a lot of the time
- some of the time
- none of the time

Question 2:
Do you have any unpaid bills?

- a lot
- some
- none

Now it's time to score.

Any question that got an "a lot" answer earns zero points.
Any question that got a "some" answer earns five points.
Any question that got a "none" answer earns ten points.

A score of twenty means you *do* have risk capacity.

Congratulations! You are officially cleared for investing.

(Fig. 12.1)

Any other score means you failed.

There, there, now. Breathe. Let it go.

(Fig. 12.2)

Sorry if that scoring took you by surprise, but I really needed to get your attention on this one. Read on for the rationale.

Question 1:

If you carefully budget your funds and find that everything is spent at the end of the month, you're not ready for the investing game. If you find that you are in the red at the end of the month, then you're *really* not ready for the investing game. Living hand-to-mouth with no savings cushion of any sort puts your risk capacity at zero.

Question 2:

You need to get your bills paid off before you start investing. I'm not talking about big-ticket items like mortgages or car payments that are already on a monthly installment plan (and rarely paid for in cash). I'm referring to credit card debt, student loan debt, or any other consumer debt. Any extra money you have needs to go toward getting those balances cleared out first. Some might say, "But Kathy, why can't I put money toward my monthly credit card bill *and* my investments? What's wrong with contributing to them at the same time?" I actually don't need to answer this question myself because an objective-free calculation provides the answer. Most credit cards charge around 15% interest. Unless your investments can provide a constant, reliable monthly return that is *greater* than 15%, your money is not being put to its most efficient use. (Oh, for crying out loud, why am I sugar-coating this? Let me rephrase—unless your investments can provide a constant, reliable monthly return that is greater than 15%, then you are pretty much **flushing your money down the pooper.**)

Don't extend the life of your debt and add on more interest charges just to put a little money in the market right now. The market will still be there for you once you're debt-free.

You will find some differing opinions on this, but I don't recognize a middle ground with risk capacity. You can't have "medium" risk capacity for the same reason that you can't be "a little bit pregnant." Either you have funds available to use for investing or you don't. (On a similar note, I wonder if I could invent a stick that you pee on to test your risk capacity? I'd be quite the sensation on *Shark Tank*.)

If you don't have risk capacity right now, it's OK. You just need to start working on it. Lots of people are in the same situation, and through budgeting and planning, you will soon have yourself a little nest egg that you can put to work for you.

Now, as for risk tolerance, you can find out where you fall on the spectrum by taking another quiz.

1. You invest $100 in CheezDoodle, Inc. During your first week as a shareholder, the stock price drops 10%. What do you do?

   1. Stay the course. You're sure that the price will bounce back eventually.
   2. Start looking for other investments in case the CheezDoodle price falls any further.
   3. Sell the stock immediately.

2. You're betting on the roll of a single die. An even number means that you will win $1000. How much would you be willing to bet on a single roll?

   1. $1
   2. $100
   3. $500
   4. Nothing

3. Your ideal investments would be:

   1. High-risk, but with the possibility of high returns.
   2. Safe with stable returns.
   3. I don't know what you are talking about. My money is under my mattress.

Now to see how well you did:

Question 1: If you can remain firm when stock prices waver, then you definitely have risk tolerance. (This isn't always easy; remember the wild peaks and valleys of the historical index charts?) If, on the other hand, you want to sell your investments the minute you see a downturn, then you have little or no risk tolerance.

Question 2: This bet has 50/50 odds of winning. When the risk is low (possibly losing $1) lots of people will probably bet. When the risk is higher (possibly losing $100), then you get a chance to see who has risk tolerance and who doesn't. Willingness to bet $500 shows extremely high risk tolerance. Reluctance to bet even a dollar shows almost no risk tolerance at all.

Question 3: You need nerves of steel to put your all of your money into high-risk investments. Only those with absurdly high levels of risk tolerance can do this. People with a medium level of risk tolerance tend to put their money in safer investments so they have a reasonable expectation of their future earnings. If you're still keeping your money under your mattress, then you have no ability to tolerate risk whatsoever.

There's no scoring for this quiz because there's no "right" amount of risk tolerance. On its own, it is equally fine to have lots of it or none of it. The more important issue at hand is ensuring that a person's risk tolerance and risk capacity are working in sync.

For example, say that "Franz" lives on risk and the rush that it brings. He is always thinking that he can flip a dollar into a fortune, whether it's buying lotto tickets, betting on horses, or investing in high-risk stocks. That's just peachy for Franz, provided that he has enough money to indulge in this kind of behavior and still stay financially afloat. In the case that he has limitless risk tolerance, but no risk capacity? Well, that's just a recipe for disaster.

Conversely, let's say that "Ferdinand" sleeps on top of his money every night—a stash that now totals one million dollars. While that shows a rather high *capacity* for risk, the fact that he is keeping his cash at home says that he doesn't have risk tolerance at all. While Ferdinand certainly has the money to invest (giving him lots of risk capacity), he shouldn't go against his gut and invest based on that fact alone. It may not make sense to the rest of us, but there's nothing wrong with having high risk capacity and low risk tolerance. Different strokes, folks.

I'll say for myself that I don't have much risk tolerance at all. I think long and hard before putting a quarter in a slot machine. One time I went to Las Vegas and racked up a $17 credit on one of the machines. I immediately cashed out and bought myself some fridge magnets and this totally authentic-looking sheriff's badge. It was a great purchase, and I was completely satisfied, because I worked right up to the limit of my risk tolerance. Never once did I think about what I "could have won" if I had stayed and continued to play.

It's a big job.

(Fig. 12.3)

You might be able to better pinpoint your feelings toward risk by studying this chart:

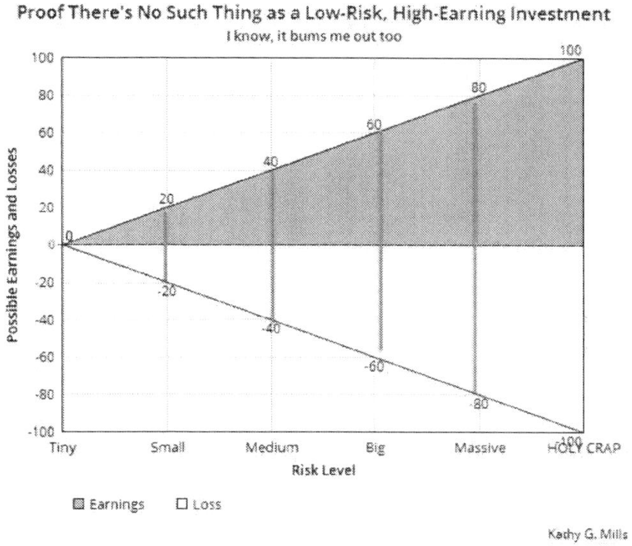

(Fig. 12.4)

Start at point "0" on the left side of the chart. At that point, zero dollars are invested, so there is no possibility of earning returns. This approach could be characterized by someone who keeps his money in his sock drawer. He won't lose the money, but he won't make any profits on it, either.

Stay on that line and slide over to the right until you get to the intersection of "0" and "small." This point shows an investment in stocks that carries a small amount of risk. The amount of possible earnings (the dark grey area above the '"0") is equal to the amount of possible loss (the white area below the "0"). You could make money or lose money at this level of investment, but either way, it probably wouldn't have a huge impact on your financial future. Would you feel most comfortable on this end of the chart?

If you have the nerve to keep sliding right all the way to the end of the chart, you'll move into the "holy crap" level of risk. At this level of investment, your earning potential, as well as your loss potential, is huge. Making or losing money at this level could very well make or break your financial fortunes. Could you operate at this end of the spectrum?

I'll bet that you, like most people, would fall somewhere in the middle of the chart. While your tendencies may run aggressive or conservative, it is unlikely that you would invest at one of the extremes like "tiny" or "holy crap." Still, finding that sweet spot can be tricky. It's all a matter of balance that feels right to you. We'll study this idea of balance further in the next chapter.

Vocabulary

Flushing your money down the pooper: Wasting your money on products, experiences, or investments that do not provide the user with a return equal to or greater than the amount of money spent. Some well-known ways to flush your money down the pooper include buying lottery tickets, subscribing to expensive cable packages, and purchasing new cars right off the showroom floor.

Risk capacity: How much money a person has to spend as disposable income without negatively affecting his bottom line. Risk capacity is different for every person.

Risk tolerance: The ability to partake in events that do not have a known outcome. This is a tendency that is also different for every person.

"Denial" Is a River in Egypt, but "Diversification" Is a Lake in Papua New Guinea

The definition of **diversification** is fairly simple—it means a mix of different things. In this chapter, you are going to learn how to use it as an investing strategy that will improve your chances of earning profits while limiting the possibility of loss. I think the topic is best expressed in terms of a whimsical riddle. So here's another story to entertain you and help illustrate the concept of diversification.

You have an egg business. You deliver eggs to the local market every day where you are paid for each fresh egg that arrives in perfect condition. Obviously, keeping the eggs safe is a priority for you; the more perfect eggs you deliver, the more money you get.

Quick note: the eggs you collect and deliver are from the long-beaked echidna.

(Fig. 13.1)

Here's the problem. The local market is across the lake. The only way you can get the eggs there is to put them in a canoe and paddle across the water.

Seems agreeable enough . . .
(Fig. 13.2)

But wait! There is an egg-loving crocodile in the lake. He has no interest in humans, but boy, does he love eggs. He always shows up four times in a twenty-four hour period looking for a canoe full of eggs. No one can predict exactly when he will appear; he's as mysterious as he is vicious.

Unfortunately for you, echidna eggs are his favorite.
(Fig. 13.3)

You have to make your delivery ASAP because eggs expire quickly in the heat (your egg business is in **Papua New Guinea**). You need to get them across the lake and over to the market as soon as you can or they'll go bad and be worthless. However, you'll always run the risk of having your canoe overturned by the crocodile and losing all your eggs. How can you deliver *as many eggs as possible* while keeping your risk of crocodile encounters to a *minimum*?

Now, I'm going to stop you right here before you get all smart-alecky on me. Don't tell me that you're going to create a special catapult to send the eggs over to the market, or that you're going to deliver them with a drone, or that you're going to hollow out pineapples and hide the eggs in there when you take them across the lake. (Besides, everyone knows that crocodiles have an excellent sense of smell.) This is my story, so just take it at face value.

Here are some possibilities:

Plan A

Just wing it. Pile up the canoe with all of your eggs, set off on the lake, and hope that the crocodile is taking a nap.

Pros: You only have to make one trip per day.

Cons: If caught, you'll lose everything.

Plan B

Make a ridiculous number of trips across the lake every day. In fact, just take *one egg* with you each time you go.

Pros: Your exposure to risk is greatly, greatly, greatly reduced.

Cons: You're spending all of your time on trips, leaving you no time for anything else. Also, you can't really make any money by selling one egg at a time.

Plan C
Make several trips a day, taking a portion of eggs with you during each trip.

Pros: Additional canoe trips limit your exposure to risk. In the event that you get canoe-jacked, you'll only lose a portion of your assets.

Cons: You will lose some eggs at some point.

You may be wondering, "What does this have to do with the stock market?" I'll make that part crystal clear, as I am wont to speak in parables, and what is a parable without an instructional lesson at the end of it?[1]

Eggs = money
Canoe trips = companies in which to invest
Crocodile = risk

Plans A, B, and C represent different ways that investors try to put their money into the stock market while managing risk (also known as **risk mitigation**).

Plan A is an investor who believes very strongly in one particular stock. This plan fails to heed the classic "too many eggs in one basket" warning, but that doesn't necessarily mean that it couldn't work. This plan has no diversity and a huge amount of risk. Only someone with a very high risk tolerance could invest this way.

Plan B is an investor who does things in the opposite way. He wants to avoid risk at all costs, so he tries to put his money into as many different investments as possible. With just small amounts invested across a broad spectrum of stocks, the investor is well protected against loss, but he also reduces his earning potential because it's hard to make money on just one or two shares of stock. This plan might appeal to someone with low or no risk tolerance.

Plan C is an investor who evaluates the options and tries to strike a balance between risk and reward. He doesn't believe in just one stock, nor does he over-diversify. This plan works for people who are somewhere in the middle range of risk tolerance.

Even though plans A and C represent different ends of the investing spectrum, they both operate based on the same faulty principle; they view egg delivery as a game that they can *win*. The person who uses Plan A is trying to time things perfectly so that he achieves a 100% delivery rate with just one trip. The person using Plan C is making excessive trips across the lake so he can achieve the lowest possible loss rate. The practitioners of these plans place too much emphasis on "beating the crocodile." Rather than accepting its presence in the lake as a fact of life, they devise elaborate and risky schemes to thwart it and end up creating new problems. They either expose themselves to dangerous and unnecessary levels of risk (as shown with Plan A) or they allow an obsessive aversion to loss to dominate their every waking moment (as shown in Plan C). This parable should make it clear that when it comes to investing, avoiding risk through extreme measures isn't an effective approach. Rather than continually scheming and trying to "win the game," it is more prudent and practical to simply accept the crocodile's presence as a factor that influences egg deliveries.

The next chapter will demonstrate some concrete examples of investor behavior, showing how Plans A, B, and C would work with real money and real stocks instead of eggs and canoes. We'll still be trying to find answers to the same questions, though.

- How can we invest our money so our earning potential is maximized?
- How can we protect our money so it isn't lost on bad investments?
- How will risk capacity and risk tolerance influence our decisions?

[1]Just a long pointless story, sometimes with talking animals.

Vocabulary

Diversification: Spreading something out (in this case, investments) so that the assets are not concentrated in any one stock. Instead, the money is distributed among multiple stocks to increase earning possibilities while managing risk.

Papua New Guinea: An independent state in the South Pacific where a nomadic people called the Meakambut live in caves. Diversity abounds, particularly when it comes to languages—more than 800 are spoken there.

Risk mitigation: A way to manage the risk associated with investing. Investors often try to mitigate risk by diversifying their holdings. They try to include companies from different sectors, as well as companies of different sizes with different risk levels. In the event that a few companies experience a drop in share prices, investments in other companies will balance out the losses.

I'm Gonna Pop Some Stocks, Got Twenty Dollars in My Pocket

Now it's time to go stock shopping. You're going to start with $1,000 and figure out what shares to purchase based on your personal investing criteria. When you're done, these shares will be referred to collectively as a **portfolio**.

Collective nouns are fun. Here are some of my favorite ones:

(Fig. 14.1)

(Fig. 14.2)

(Fig. 14.3)

I know it's not a contest or anything, but an "implausibility of gnus" is the clear winner here.

If your brokerage account is set up, this process is exactly like any other online shopping experience. Cruise through the site for a product that interests you, check the price, and then pop it into your shopping cart. When you're ready to check out, click the "submit order" button and you're all done. No need for a professional to do the purchasing for you, and really, no need to know anything about what you're investing in. (I don't recommend that as a strategy, btw. Just pointing out that stock purchasing is remarkably easy.)

Here are some different ways you could invest $1,000: The first one is called:

The "I Totally Love This Company" Portfolio

Name	Sector	Size	Risk level	# of shares	Price
Beepy!	Gaming	Mid cap	Medium	11	$88
Subtotal					$968
Fees					$10
Total					$978

You can't beat this portfolio for simplicity, but it's clear that there's no element of risk mitigation. On the other hand, it presents a unique opportunity for the savvy (or maybe just lucky) investor. If you have reason to believe that a stock is going to explode in value someday, or if you just enjoy rolling the dice and taking a chance, putting all of your money in one stock could be the way to go. As long as that kind of investment matches your risk capacity and risk tolerance, there's no compelling reason not to try.

Do you ever think about going back in time and investing in all of the companies that you know will turn out to be winners? I do that a lot. If I had to pick just one stock to invest in after stepping out of a time machine, I think it would be Amazon. After the dot.com bust in the early 2000s, Amazon shares dropped to a record low of $5.97. If I'd had the foresight to put $1,000 into Amazon and the willpower to keep the stock until today, my investment would look like this:

2001		**2017**	
165 shares @ 5.97	$985.05	165 shares @ 976.62	$161,142.30
Fees	$10	Minus investment of	-$995.05
Total Investment	$995.05	**Profit**	**$160,147.25**

You could also let the pendulum swing all the way to the other side. Instead of pinning your hopes and dreams on just one stock, you could invest in a much larger cross-section of stocks. I'll call this:

The Super-Duper Diversified Portfolio

Name	**Sector**	**Size**	**Risk level**	**# of shares**	**Price**
Drugzzz	Pharmacy	Large cap	Low	1	$116
Gloop	Industrial materials	Large cap	Low	1	$104
Kibbly	Snacks	Large cap	Low	1	$101
Vroom	Auto maker	Mid cap	Medium	1	$98
Beads	Jewelry	Mid cap	Medium	1	$92
Flair Wear	Apparel	Mid cap	Medium	1	$87
Beepy	Gaming	Mid cap	Medium	1	$88
Chip Heads	Tech	Small cap	High	1	$40
SkyPower	Airline	Small cap	High	1	$26
FluZeez	Biotech	Small cap	High	1	$52
Subtotal					$892
Fees					$100
Total					$992

This portfolio owns one share each of ten different companies. Each company represents a different sector of the economy, and there is an even mix of large, medium and small cap companies. This collection demonstrates an understanding of risk mitigation. In the case that one or two of the companies experience a steep drop in prices, investments in other companies will keep the portfolio healthy.

But the extent of diversification presents challenges as well. Trying to buy into as many companies as possible on a $1,000 budget usually means you can't afford more than one share of each company. Do you know how long it will take to earn money on just one share of stock? For example, if Gloop Co. publishes its quarterly statement and reports a gain of 1.2% (which is by all accounts average for that time frame), then you've just made yourself a whopping $1.25. Even if it experienced an extraordinary (and unlikely) 10% jump, you would still just make $10.40, which is barely enough to cover the cost of purchasing the share.

And while we're on the topic of transaction fees, remember that buying one share of each of these companies counts as ten separate transactions. That means you pay the $10 fee ten times for a total of $100—a full 10% of your budget. Diversification can be expensive.

I'm not saying that it is a waste of time to start investing this way. After all, everyone has to start somewhere. I just want your expectations to be realistic. Making money on this portfolio is entirely doable, provided that you 1) add to your shares as often as you can and 2) practice monumental, almost biblical patience.

You could also construct a portfolio that lies somewhere between these two extreme approaches. I call it:

The Safe Bet Portfolio

Name	Sector	Size	Risk level	# of shares	Price
Nike	$44.64	Large cap	Low	6	$287.84
Apple	$125.68	Large cap	Low	2	$251.36
Marriott	$89.50	Large cap	Low	3	$268.50
WWE	$20.52	Large cap	Low	7	$143.64
Subtotal					$951.34
Fees					$40
Total					$991.34

This portfolio looks promising. It doesn't include as many companies as the super-duper diversified portfolio, but it still manages to cover different sectors that are vital to the economy: apparel (Nike), tech (Apple), hotels (Marriott), and wrestling (WWE). This smaller collection also limits your transaction fees to a moderate $40. These large cap stocks will most likely remain stable and earn money over time, meaning you have a reasonable expectation for steady, albeit modest earnings. Plus—having a few shares of each will multiply your earnings and you'll see profits sooner. This portfolio will still take some time to earn a profit, so don't start talking through your teeth with a **Thurston Howell III** accent just yet.

I find it interesting to think about how these companies, because of the important role they play in my financial planning, affect my life in such a personal way. In the event that WWE stock blows up, I would have the pride and satisfaction of knowing that this guy. . .

(Fig. 14.4)

. . .is directly involved in securing a comfortable retirement for my loved ones and me.

Although these three portfolios demonstrate very different approaches to investing, they do have one thing in common. They were all constructed by the process of **stock picking**. I know—that seems completely obvious. You picked the stocks, so of course you call it stock picking. But this process needs a name so that it can be distinguished from other methods of investing. You see, there is another way to secure a complete portfolio—one that is diverse and balanced by size, risk level and sector—and all you have to do is buy one little share of stock.

I know you're dying to find out what it is, but since I've got you where I want you, I'll just slip another quiz in here. Go on—give it a try. You'll be glad you did.

Vocabulary

Portfolio: A collection of stocks. A portfolio could contain just a few shares of one company or multiple shares of many different companies.

Stock picking: The process of identifying individual stocks and purchasing them to create a hand-picked portfolio.

Thurston Howell III: The fabulously wealthy old coot who took a doomed trip on the *SS Minnow* with Gilligan and the gang. My favorite character because somehow, even though he was stranded on an uninhabited island, he always managed to produce a bottle of champagne in the evenings.

QUIZ 3

1. Who is in the best position to determine your risk tolerance?
    a. Your broker
    b. Your banker
    c. Your congressman
    d. YOU

2. Trading is an example of "set and forget" investing.
    a. True
    b. False

3. Select the answer that shows three different sectors in which to invest.
    a. Tech, energy, computers
    b. Apple, GE, BlueCross
    c. Microsoft, Apple, Dell
    d. Tech, energy, healthcare

4. Why do traders buy and sell so often?
    a. They drink a lot of Red Bull.
    b. They want to increase their chances of big returns.
    c. They want to avoid losses and increase their returns.
    d. They want to avoid risk at all cost.

5. Diversification eliminates the risk of loss.
    a. True
    b. False

6. One of the main differences between investors and traders is:
    a. Investors deal in stocks, traders deal in cash and products.
    b. Traders buy and sell frequently; investors buy and hold.
    c. An investor's goal is to increase earnings; a trader's goal is to increase transactions per day.
    d. Traders buy and hold; investors buy and sell frequently.

7. Stock picking doesn't have to be done by a broker; anyone can do it.
    a. True
    b. False

8. Stock picking requires extensive study before you can buy stocks.
    a. True
    b. False

9. What is the most convincing argument for diversifying your investments?
    a. Diverse holdings mitigate risk and losses.
    b. Diverse holdings increase your chances of finding a stock with big returns.
    c. Diverse holdings have higher returns overall.
    d. Diverse holdings allow you to refer to yourself as a "stock baron."

10. John has massive risk capacity and an opportunity to invest in a new company—Jiggle Java. It manufactures a highly-caffeinated, coffee-flavored gelatin snack. Jiggle Java expects massive growth and earnings in the coming months and finance pundits are declaring it the "next big thing" in gelatinized coffee products. What should John do?
    a. Invest all of the money he has available to him. Chances like this come along once in a lifetime.
    b. Talk to his broker and ask how much money he should invest.
    c. Invest if he believes in the product and feels comfortable putting his money in stocks.
    d. Buy as much stock as possible and sell as soon as the price drops.

11. Why pick the stocks for your portfolio? Choose the best answer:
    a. Picking your own stocks gives you more control over your holdings.
    b. Picking your own stocks is cheaper.
    c. Picking your own stocks doesn't require a broker.
    d. Picking your own stocks is the only way to diversify.

12. It is possible to have no risk capacity and unlimited risk tolerance.
    a. True
    b. False

13. What is another difference between investors and traders?
    a. Investors can make money in up or down markets; traders usually can't.
    b. Investors stick to the tech sector; traders buy and sell in any sector.
    c. Traders can make money in up or down markets; investors usually can't.
    d. Investors sell stocks in a market downturn; traders keep them.

14. Why is the long-billed echidna special?
    a. It is an egg-laying mammal.
    b. It is a warm-blooded reptile.
    c. It is an amphibian with porcupine-like spikes.
    d. It lays black eggs.

15. Fees to buy stocks from an online broker are based on the total amount of your investment.
    a. True
    b. False

Answer Key to Quiz 3

1. D

   I hope you didn't waver on this one. Though really, if your congressman knows you well enough to weigh in on your investment choices, I'd say you have a darn good congressman.

2. B

   Investing is a set and forget method.

3. D

   Choice "A" doesn't work because "tech" and "computers" are the same category. Choices "B" and "C" name companies, not sectors.

4. C

   The traders are trying to have it all—big returns with no losses.

5. B

   You can never eliminate risk.

6. B

   Traders are like the hare—they're always moving.

7. A

   It's true—anyone can do it. That doesn't mean that just anyone can be good at it, though.

8. B

   You can pick stocks without knowing a darn thing about them, and many people do. This may or may not work out well for you.

9. A

   But go ahead and call yourself a "stock baron." No one is going to call you on it.

10. C

    But *don't* try to go out and start your own Jiggle Java. I've already got a patent on that name.

11. A

    While answers "B" and "C" are often true, they are not the best reasons on this list. Picking your own stocks gives you more control as an investor.

12. A

    This is totally possible, and it's a recipe for disaster.

13. C

    Remember that traders never miss an opportunity to make a buck.

14. A

    I know I didn't explicitly cover this in the chapters, but really, don't you have any natural curiosity? I just assumed you read up on the echidna as soon as you had a chance.

15. B

    The fee is normally charged per trade. It will vary from brokerage to brokerage, but at the moment runs anywhere between $5 and $20.

If you did well on this quiz, it means that you are now prepared to evaluate stocks and other potential investments based on your personal investing criteria. That is a major step forward in acquiring your Market Mojo. In fact, your Mojo tank is starting to get full. Top it off by finishing Part Four.

Part 4

Planning a Personal Portfolio

Don't Be Mutually Exclusive
Index Funds: Practicality Meets Profitability
Exchange Traded Fund? More Like Exchange Traded FUN!
Ti—-iiiime . . . Is on Your Side (Yes It Is!)

Planning a Personal Portfolio

The last section of the book will introduce you to another important investing option—funds. Funds are just plain *nifty*. Investing in them is easy and often very cost-effective, and they provide you with instant diversification just by purchasing one little share. They make a fabulous addition to any portfolio, offering exposure to earning possibilities as well as risk mitigation. If you are a little turned off by the outlay of money and time needed to build a portfolio solely through stock picking, then you will be thrilled to learn how funds can simplify this process.

Don't Be Mutually Exclusive

I'm sure you've heard the term **mutual funds** before. If you don't entirely understand how mutual funds work, you're not alone. I took an informal poll among my friends at a recent get-together, asking them how they were saving for retirement. While nearly everyone answered, "We have mutual funds," I couldn't get anyone to explain to me exactly what mutual funds are or how they work. Maybe they really had no idea. Maybe they were afraid of being wrong and sounding stupid. Or maybe they didn't want to discuss finances at a party and figured if they shrugged and smiled, I would stop questioning them. That's unfortunate, because mutual funds really are easy to understand, and you should know how they fit into an overall investing picture.

Say you've saved up $1,000 and you're ready to invest it. You understand your risk tolerance and risk capacity, and you know that you need to have some diversification in your holdings. The problem is, you're not too keen on doing the research and figuring out which stocks to invest in. You wish that someone would just put a mix of promising and high-earning stocks into a shopping cart for you and say, "Here—these are the ones you want."

You could certainly do that, but then you would have another problem on your hands. One share each of all of the stocks in the cart comes to $5,862. You only have $1,000, remember? It appears it is impossible to buy the entire contents of the cart today. You'll just have to save your money and be patient . . .or *will* you?

Maybe not. Did you know there's a sneaky little shortcut you can use to buy everything in that cart with your $1,000? All it takes is a little . . .

(Fig. 1.4)

Like most magic tricks, this one seems impossible until someone explains it to you—then it makes perfect sense. A mutual fund is a collective fund that is managed by a financial professional called a **fund manager**. A mutual fund manager is responsible for finding other people just like you—folks who want to invest, but are working with a limited amount of money. By pooling *everyone's* money together, the manager has a significant amount of capital that can be used to purchase a diversified selection of stocks—a selection that normally would be out of the price range of an average investor.

This kind of collective buying isn't a new idea, and it isn't limited to stock purchases. Have you ever heard a story about a group of coworkers pooling their money to buy lottery tickets? Why do you think they do that? They want to get as many tickets as possible by spending the least amount of money. If a ticket costs $1 and 100 people purchase 100 tickets as a group, then it's a great deal for everyone. Each person has access to 100 tickets and only had to pay a dollar for that privilege.

The "catch" is that no one person owns all 100 tickets. An individual only owns a tiny sliver of each ticket, just like all of the other coworkers. If one of those 100 tickets wins the $10 million prize, the money will be spread out evenly among all of the investors. It's still a great deal though—everyone wins $100,000 for making an investment of just one dollar.

The distribution of funds can change depending on the number of participants and the different level of investments. In the previous example, everyone contributed the same amount of money, so they were able to share in the prize money equally. But that's just one way to collectively invest. Another way would be this: I enter into a similar agreement with 49 of my coworkers. They all contribute $1 each to purchase 49 tickets for the pool. I contribute $51 and contribute 51 tickets to the pool, bringing the total to 100 tickets for the entire group. If one of those tickets wins the $10 million prize, I'll get 51% of the winnings because my investment represented 51% of the money used to buy the tickets. The other 49 coworkers will equally share 49% of the prize money between them. It's profitable for everyone; I get $5,100,000 for my $51 investment, and each of my coworkers will get $100,000 for their $1 investment.

I should point out that I am *not* advocating playing the lottery as your investment strategy. Even if you win, look what it does to some people. You don't see mutual fund owners acting like this when they get a big return.

(Fig. 15.1)

In a general sense, a mutual fund works the same way. It collects money from lots of investors, and then uses the money to purchase many shares of stock from various companies in different sectors. When the fund makes money, the earnings are divided proportionally among the investors. It's a great way to get access to hundreds, or even thousands of stocks that you as an individual investor would never be able to afford on your own.

There are oodles of different mutual funds to choose from. Each one is designed to meet a particular investing goal. Want to try making a lot of money in a short period of time by investing in high-risk stocks? There's a mutual fund for that. Want a portfolio of perfectly balanced holdings with some risky and some not-so-risky investments? There's a mutual fund for that. Want to invest in only the safest investments possible? (All together now . . .) *There's a mutual fund for that.*

There are even **ethical mutual funds**. If you want to put money into a fund that doesn't have any holdings in or connection to gambling, alcohol, or cigarettes, you can find it. Likewise, there are an equal number of **sin funds** out there that almost exclusively deal in the racy stuff.

(Fig. 15.2)

Managing a mutual fund is a huge responsibility. Not only does the fund manager personally curate the fund by selecting the most promising stocks, he must also ensure that the fund is appropriately balanced by spreading the holdings out among different companies and sectors. Furthermore, he must continually adjust the fund by selling shares before they drop in value and purchasing affordable shares before they increase in price. A crystal ball isn't required to be a fund manager, but it sure wouldn't hurt. A big part of the job is making predictions about how stocks will behave and then buying or selling accordingly. When you invest in a managed mutual fund, you not only get instant diversification, but you save yourself time by leaving all of the hard work of stock picking to someone else.

Are you arching an eyebrow now and saying, "How much extra do I have to pay to use a fund manager?" If so, then good for you. That shows you have the makings of a savvy investor and you truly understand the meaning of the phrase "Ain't Nothin' Free, Baby." Using a fund manager is a form of **active investing** and it is going to cost you extra in the form of an **expense ratio**. An expense ratio is a fee collected to cover the manager's salary, administrative costs, operating costs, and even advertising for the fund. A typical mutual fund expense ratio these days might cost you 1.25% of the portfolio's value at the end of every year.

In addition to the expense ratio, some mutual funds charge **load fees**. A **front-end load** fee is a charge that you pay up front when you make your initial investment. A **back-end load** fee is charged when you redeem the fund. These "loads" can cost up to 5% of the total investment.

Here's an example to really bring these numbers home. Say you have $50,000 to invest. You choose an actively managed fund called KGM Mutual. It has a 5% front-end load fee, and a yearly expense ratio of 1.25%. You earn a yearly 6% return on this investment, and you put *no* other money into the fund. Here's how much money your fund will earn at the end of three different earning periods, and the fees you'll pay to management:

Investment amount: $50,000
Front-end load fee: 5% or $2,500
Money available for investment: $47,500

By the end of year five: 66,911 in earnings (minus $3,455 in fees)
By the end of year fifteen: 119,828 in earnings (minus $13,253 in fees)
By the end of year thirty: 287,175 in earnings (minus $39,555 in fees)

At the end of thirty years, you will have paid out an astounding $40,000 for that 1.25% expense ratio. And here's a fun little kicker—even if the fund *loses* money, management will still get its expense ratio payment. Consider that for a moment. Does it make you feel a little . . . oh, I don't know . . . skeptical?

This is Business Kitty. He can be a little cynical, but he often makes some excellent points.
(Fig. 15.3)

You may counter my argument with: "So what if I have to pay extra fees? That's why I have a manager. I'm going to find a guy who will *crush* the market, and I'll make so much money, it won't matter how much I have to pay in fees."

Well . . . no. That probably won't happen. I'm not just being cautious or trying to manage your expectations. It turns out that actively managed funds don't do better than non-managed funds. In fact, most of them do a lot worse.

A fifteen-year market study that concluded in December of 2016 found that 92 to 95% of actively managed mutual funds did NOT even reach the benchmarks set by non-managed funds. (SPIVA, 2017) You don't have to be a professional bookie to know that those odds *stink*.

In the final analysis, is a managed mutual fund a good fit for your portfolio? The good news is that it allows for diversification with a small up-front investment. The bad news is that managed funds charge fees that can dramatically reduce your overall earnings. This doesn't mean that you should entirely rule out the idea of putting your money in a managed mutual fund, but it does mean that you should read the fine print carefully, making sure that you understand the expense ratio and any other associated fees.

In the next chapter, you'll learn about a special kind of mutual fund. It gets reliable returns and the expense ratios are super-low. I think it takes the model of the mutual fund and vastly improves upon it so that it is an attractive option for just about any kind of investor.

Vocabulary

Active investing: Using the services of a professional financial manager. Most active investing takes place through actively-managed mutual funds.

Back end load: A fee charged when you sell your mutual fund. It is usually expressed as a percentage of the value of the fund.

Ethical mutual funds: Mutual funds that do not invest in any companies that are considered (by some) to be peddling vice (cigarettes, alcohol, gambling, etc.). Funds that deal almost exclusively in these companies are called "sin funds."

Expense ratio: A fee charged for actively managed funds. These fees vary, but can cost between 1% and 2% of the total value of the fund annually.

Front-end load: A fee charged up-front to buy a mutual fund. It is usually expressed as a percentage of the total amount to be invested.

Load fees: Fees charged when purchasing or redeeming shares of a mutual fund.

Mutual funds: An investment tool created by a manager who pools the money of many different investors and then uses the combined funds to establish a portfolio made up of different kinds of stocks. This provides an option to buy into several companies at once with the purchase of just one share. When the fund earns money, the profits are split proportionally among the fund holders.

Index Funds: Practicality Meets Profitability

A "mutual fund" is something of an umbrella term because it can describe any collective fund that contains the stocks of many different companies. The mutual funds we learned about in the last chapter are managed by fund managers who continually update and adjust the collection in order to get the best possible return for their investors. We also learned that these funds can be expensive and that they rarely outperform any other funds.

If that doesn't sound like such a great deal to you, then you might be interested in index funds. Index funds are a kind of mutual fund because they are a collection of stocks. But unlike mutual funds, they don't have managers.

How can a fund survive without a manager, you ask? Easy—instead of engaging in stock picking to create the portfolio, the fund only invests in the stocks of one particular index. That's what makes it an **index fund**. If you buy an S&P index fund, that means that you own shares of every company listed on the S&P. If you buy a Nasdaq index fund, you own shares of every company listed on the Nasdaq. And if you buy into the Dow Jones index fund, then you own shares of all 30 stocks listed on the Dow.

Index funds have so many advantages. Here they are in a quick list that I'm sure you'll want to print and tack up on your fridge for reference:

- You don't need to know a thing about stocks to invest in an index fund. If you like the companies in the DJIA, then you can have them. All you need to do is buy shares of an index fund that follows the DJIA.

- It's easy to know how your portfolio is doing at any given time. The stock quotes you hear on the news for the indices will tell you (plus or minus a few points) how your fund is performing.
- Index funds have very, very low expense ratios because there's no fund manager. In fact, computers do the majority of the work that keeps index funds running. No manager working on the fund = (almost) no fees. This is known as **passive investing**.
- Index funds offer risk mitigation through instant diversification.
- Index funds do *not* try to beat the market. They try to stay in step with the market.

Regarding that last bullet point, you may be thinking to yourself, "How is that a selling point? I don't want to settle for *average* market returns. I want to *beat* the market—that's why I'm investing."

Well yes, I see your point. On the face of it, that seems like a logical reaction. But if you take a closer look at the strategies you would use to beat the market, you may change your tune.

1. Stock picking: It's you against the market. You need to identify the most promising companies, judge their worth, and determine which ones to buy or sell at the perfect time. You don't know anything about how to make these determinations. Whoops!
Verdict: You will lose money.

2. Stock picking with help: You decide to pick stocks by consulting the "hot tip" websites—the ones that claim to know all of the "secrets" to beating the market. (Are you taking note of my gratuitous and sarcastic use of quotation marks?) These sites will almost always charge a hefty membership fee to use their services. After getting that fee, they don't have any real incentive to try to make good stock picks for you. (Not that they know how, anyway.)
Verdict: You will lose money.

3. Identifying just one awesome stock at the perfect time and putting all your money in it: Some companies make history. Amazon, for example, has seen its stock price increase 48,197% since its IPO. (Hoffman, 2017) Wow! But the probability of *you* identifying a new company that achieves a similar feat? One chance in a bazillion.
Verdict: You will lose money.

4. Get an actively managed fund: Buy into a fund that is overseen by a professional—a guy who promises that *his* stock picks will build the most profitable fund ever. There are actually two possibilities if you decide to go this route.

1. The fund *does* make some great earnings. You then proceed to hand over those earnings to the fund manager and the company he works for to cover the administrative costs and other associated fees.
   Verdict: Net profit of 0
2. The fund tanks and you lose money. To add insult to injury, you still have to pay the fancy-pants fund manager for his time.
   Verdict: You will lose money.

See what I mean? It turns out that "beating the market" isn't as realistic as you have been led to believe, and it's really not a sound approach to investing.

History has shown that the market will provide an average return of 7% to investors, provided that they hold on to their investments for the long-term. (The long-term aspect is critical because low-earning years and high-earning years balance each other out to land on that 7% figure.) (Hoffman, 2016) That may not put you into the Warren Buffett league, but most actively managed funds don't even perform *that* well. Add to that high fees and the possibility of bad management, and you'll see that actively managed funds can rob investors of significant earnings over the years.

Here are two charts that compare the earnings and fees for a $10,000 investment. The first investment is an actively-managed mutual fund, while the second is a passively-managed index fund. Both earn a respectable 6% every year with no additional investments.

Actively Managed Fund $10,000 – $500 for 5% front-end load fee = $9,500 for investment 1.25% expense ratio; 6% annual earnings			
	Earnings	**Minus Fees**	**Take Home $**
End of year 5	12,713	691	12,022
End of year 10	17,013	1,559	15,454
End of year 15	22,767	2,651	20,116
End of year 30	54,563	7,911	**46,652**

Passively Managed Fund $10,000 for investment, no load fees 0.2% expense ratio; 6% annual earnings			
	Earnings	**Minus Fees**	**Take Home $**
End of year 5	13,382	119	13,263
End of year 10	17,908	277	17,631
End of year 15	23,966	486	23,480
End of year 30	57,435	1,615	**55,820**

Are you starting to feel me now?

The impact of the 5% load fee can really be seen in the early years of these investments. Because it reduces the amount of money that can be invested, the active fund immediately trails the passive one. At the end of year five, passive earnings are already $669 ahead of active earnings. Add in the expense ratio of 1.25%, and the difference in take-home earnings during the same time period is $1,241. By the end of year thirty, the passive investor takes home $9,168 more than the active investor.

Of course, the charts above optimistically assume that the active and passive funds make the same percentage of earnings at 6%. What would those numbers look like in a more realistic setting—one in which the actively-managed fund *under-performed* compared to the market? If the actively-managed fund just managed to bring in 5%, here's what that would look like in comparison to the passively-managed fund bringing in 6%:

Actively Managed Fund $10,000 – $500 for 5% front-end load fee = $9,500 for investment 1.25% expense ratio; 5% annual earnings			
	Earnings	**Minus Fees**	**Take Home $**
End of year 5	12,125	671	11,454
End of year 10	15,475	1,476	13,999
End of year 15	19,750	2,440	17,310
End of year 30	41,058	6,639	**34,419**

Compare that to the passively-managed index fund. I'll do the math for you—at the end of year thirty, it's a difference of **$21,401**. Is anyone out there so well off that you can afford to turn your back on an extra 21Gs? (Pauses for responses). Nope, didn't think so. How about one last chart for a summary?

Active Funds	**Passive Funds**
Charge big fees Often perform below market Earn less in the long run	Charge tiny little fees Match the market Earn more in the long run

If this chapter didn't make a strong enough case for index funds, then I'll throw a final Hail Mary pass and present the conclusion of Princeton Professor of Economics, Burton Malkeil. He's been skeptical of the mutual fund experts for years, and the following amazing quote is attributed to him: *"A blindfolded monkey throwing darts at the stock listings could select a portfolio that would do just as well as one selected by the experts."* (Stein, 2016) Just imagine that for a minute:

"Hello. I'm your advisor, ***Mr. Fuzzy Nuts****. I'll be making decisions that will determine your financial future. Have a seat while I finish throwing my feces into the air and I'll be right with you."*

(Fig. 16.1)

Is this enough of a wake-up call? Not only are the experts no better than you at picking stocks, they can't even compete with Mr. Fuzzy Nuts.

I'm not going to go so far as to say that all mutual funds are bad and that all mutual fund managers are just trying to take money out of your pocket. But I *will* say that if you are considering a mutual fund, look for a no-load fund and try to get the lowest possible expense ratio that you can find. And if you manage to find that amazing actively managed mutual fund that is totally worth the fees you pay? Let me know—'cause I sure haven't found it yet.

Vocabulary

Index fund: A kind of mutual fund that is made up of all of the stocks listed on a particular index. The fees for index funds are low because they are not actively managed; most of the work on the fund is done by computers.

Mr. Fuzzy Nuts: Although Mr. Fuzzy Nuts is of unknown origin, he appears to be a type of macaque, possibly a Balinese long-tailed monkey. There is some lore regarding his stock-picking prowess, but I was not able to substantiate those claims.

Passive investing: An investment in funds that are not managed by a fund manager.

Exchange Traded Fund? More Like Exchange Traded FUN!

The last security we are going to learn about is a hybrid of all of the other investment options that we have studied. An **ETF** is an exchange traded fund, and it offers some interesting earning possibilities for the right kind of investor.

An ETF is a kind of mutual fund because it is a collection of diversified securities. An ETF is also a kind of index fund because it tracks all of the stocks on a particular index. And finally, an ETF is like a share of stock because it can be traded throughout the day on the stock exchanges.

Before you can really appreciate the unique qualities that an ETF has to offer, you need to be aware of one important fact about managed mutual funds and index funds. Those securities can only be traded *once* a day—at the close of the market. Even if you put in an order to buy shares of a mutual fund at 10:00 a.m., your broker won't be able to make the actual purchase until the end of the day. This means that people who buy the same mutual fund on the same day all pay the same price.

So?

I know . . . that's what I thought when I first started learning the difference between these securities. *Why* exactly does it matter if I get my share of the KGM mutual fund at ten o'clock in the morning or five o'clock in the evening? What would be the benefit of being able to buy and sell shares of KGM throughout the day?

To answer that, we need to think of the kind of the investors who like to keep moving—always looking to buy low, sell high, and hit all of the peaks without spending time in any of the valleys. Sound familiar?

(Fig. 11.3)

Why, it's traders, of course. Remember, these are the guys that might trade a stock three or four times a day in order to make some short-term gains. And if they enjoy trading single shares of stock throughout the day, just think about how excited they would get at the prospect of trading *entire funds* throughout the day. Instead of flipping Coca-Cola back and forth a few times in an afternoon, they could do that with hundreds, maybe thousands of stocks at once.

The price of a share of a fund changes during the day just like any other stock. Traders, then, hope to take advantage of those changes in price by buying and selling funds at just the right times to make a profit.

You'll need to do some research to determine if an ETF is a better investment for you than a regular index fund. I always look at expenses and investment minimums first when I'm making comparisons. Here's the general scoop on those:

- ETFs generally have lower expense ratios than index funds. (Of course, index fund expense ratios are already pretty darn low.)
- ETFs charge transaction fees of $8 to $10 a pop. Many index funds, on the other hand, can be purchased directly from the fund company without incurring a transaction fee at all.
- ETFs usually don't have an investment minimum.
- ETFs don't charge load fees.

But the biggest difference, in my opinion, is the experience you will have with these funds if you are a "buy and hold" type. As a natural saver, I like to make regular contributions to my accounts and continually purchase new shares—that's my **igel-like approach to building wealth**. If I have $1000 to spend on additional shares of an index fund, I can buy them directly from the fund company without incurring any commissions or fees. That is a great deal for me because all of my money is applied directly to my investment. An ETF, on the other hand, must be purchased through a brokerage account and for that reason, there is a charge every time I buy or sell a share. Traders may not mind that, but investors like me are put off. Why should I pay a trading fee for shares that I intend to keep for the haul?

It seems to me that if you are really going to make an ETF worth your while, then you need to be a *very* savvy trader. You need to know how to time your buying and selling to make gains. Not just *some* gains, but *huge* gains that can cover the high cost of trading and still provide you with a profit. If you are *not* a savvy trader, but a slow and steady investor who is playing the long game, then a regular index fund will probably be your best bet.

Vocabulary

ETF: An index fund that trades like a stock. Instead of buying or selling an ETF only once a day, an investor has the option to buy and sell ETFs throughout the day.

Igel-like approach to building wealth: This is the slow and steady way to save money for the future, as demonstrated by *der Igel* in the classic Grimm's fairy tale. An igel-like approach does not allow anyone to get rich quick. It is not an elaborate or flashy scheme. Rather, it quietly works to invest money in low-fee funds with growth potential, eventually creating significant wealth for the investor.

Ti-iiiime . . . Is on Your Side (Yes It Is!)

Now you're going to learn how to take everything you have learned so far and apply it to a **timeline**. Investing doesn't happen over the course of a few days or weeks. If you're serious about it, then it is something you are going to do over the course of your lifetime. As you go through different phases in your life, you are going to have different commitments, different demands on your disposable income, and different goals for the future. All of those phases require a different investment strategy. That's where the timeline comes in.

Going for the obvious, your timeline for investing refers to the length of time you expect to have your funds invested. If you're a young'un and you're already thinking about investing, you have lots of earning years ahead of you. Good for you for taking this important step in securing your financial future at such a young age.

If you are a bit long in the tooth, as they say, then your timeline is much shorter. Perhaps time has slipped by you, and you are just now getting around to figuring out how the whole "investing thing" works. No worries—it happens. Besides, even though you may not have a lot of money saved up, I'm sure you have lots of the other benefits that come with age. You're probably regarded as a respected elder in your village, or maybe you can tell when it's going to rain because your "knee is acting up again."

Depending on your age, you might expect to have fifty years for your money to be cranking in the Wall Street system, or you might only have five. It doesn't matter, since there's nothing you can do about that number now. You just need to figure out what it is so you can move on to the next step—**allocation**.

Allocation is easy—it refers to how things are divided. For example, all of us are given twenty-four hours in a day, and we all allocate them to different activities. What activities do you spend your time on? How much time do you give to each activity?

My allocation of time is pretty simple these days. Monday through Friday, I sleep nine hours a night (though I wish it were ten), and I work nine and a half hours a day. Those remaining five and a half hours are divided between eating, practicing my accordion, writing, and watching all eight seasons of the medical drama *House*. I can't get enough of that irascible, curmudgeonly doctor who thumbs his nose at convention and plays by his own rules. And like all women who have a galloping crush on a complete A-hole, I always think to myself, "But I could *change* him. I could show him how to love."

This guy currently occupies about 8% of my time portfolio.
(Fig. 17.1)

Younger folks are generally advised to allocate their funds differently from the older crowd. There's a very simple reason for that—with more time to work with, younger folks can comfortably tolerate the ups and the downs of the market. They have *years* to ride out any stock market downturns and maybe even a meltdown or two. An older person, on the other hand, doesn't have the luxury of time. A meltdown would be disastrous when you only have five years to invest and a crash happens in year four.

For these reasons, many in the financial world have concluded that young folks should invest heavily in riskier securities (mainly stocks). Older folks with limited time in the market should focus mainly on the protection of their principal. (Which translates to safe investments like cash or other dependable options like bonds, money market accounts, or CDs.)

Look at some timeline investment options for plucky twenty-year-old Sally who is just starting to think about her financial future. You can see that the majority of her money is invested in stocks. She has time to ride the wave of market changes and take advantage of the effect that time will have on her earnings:

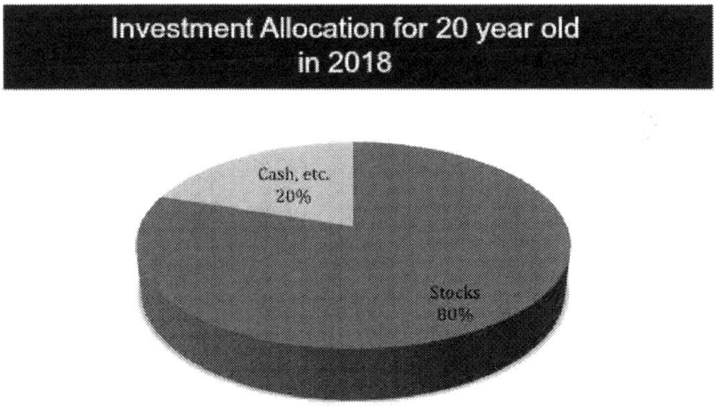

Fig. 17.2

The years pass and plucky little Sally hits the big 4-0. She decides she should re-allocate her investment funds because she doesn't have as much time in the market as she used to. She decides to take a chunk of money out of stocks and move it over into the safer investments. This is called **rebalancing**. When you rebalance a portfolio, you make adjustments to it that will keep it on track for your overall goal. In this case, the overall goal is having as much money as possible at retirement, which means taking steps to protect capital in the later years.

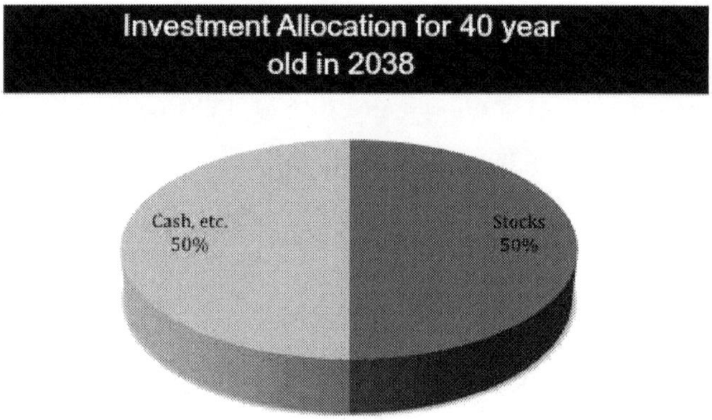

Fig. 17.3

Twenty years later, when Sally gets close to retirement, she does a review of her investments. She's awfully proud of her track record—taking advantage of the stock market all the way back in 2018 to make some gains, and then gradually moving her money into safer investments so she wasn't exposed to as much risk as she got older. All she has to do is hang on to that pile of cash, because that's the money she's going to live on now. What will she do? Why . . . rebalance the portfolio again, of course. She'll park the majority of that money in the safe zone so she can count on it for years to come.

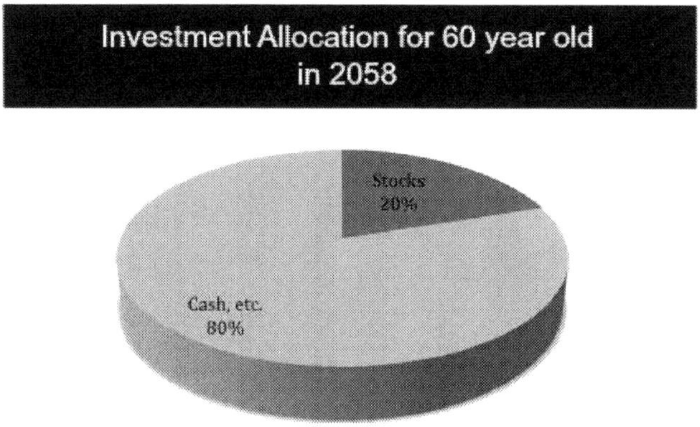

Fig. 17.4

Timeline investing, then, refers to how you allocate your money during the time you have to invest it. Generally speaking, you become more conservative with your investments the older you get. You may hear the terms "**age-based funds**" or "**target date funds**" used to describe the same investing strategy.

The target dates strategy is commonly used with college funds and retirement funds. For example, my daughter will graduate high school in the year 2020, so her college fund is actually called the "2020 fund." It invests the money we put into it exactly as you'd expect—lots in stocks during the early years, then more of it into safer investments the closer she gets to graduation. My retirement fund, called the "2035 fund" for the date I expect to retire, operates exactly the same way.

Again, there's traditional investment strategy and then there's personal strategy.

I know I have made this point before, but it bears repeating. There is no "right way" to invest—timeline investing is just one of *many* ways that you can do it. If you've done the research and you have determined that you feel better putting most of your money in cash and bonds, then by golly, you put most of your money in cash and bonds. If you decide that you want an even split between stocks and cash, then you can split your money between stocks and cash. There are a million ways to allocate funds and you can choose any one of them that you want. *You* are in the driver's seat when it comes to your portfolio.

An overeager advisor with questionable advice is a red flag.
(Fig. 17.5)

Now it's time for your final quiz!

Vocabulary

Allocation: The act of dividing things. In this case, it refers to how a portfolio is divided and how much money is allotted to different investments.

Rebalancing: The process of changing the investments in a portfolio to help keep it on target. With timeline investing, rebalancing throughout the life of the fund is necessary to ensure that earning goals are met.

Timeline investing: Investing funds according to a specific date in the future. Timeline investing is often used in retirement planning and college planning, when participants know what year they will want to cash in their funds. With timeline investing, funds are typically invested in more risky securities in the early years of the fund's life, and gradually moved over into safer investments near the end of the fund's life. This kind of investing strategy is also used in funds referred to as **target date funds** or **age-based funds**.

QUIZ 4

1. Index funds are a low-fee investing option.
    a. True
    b. False

2. What is a target date fund?
    a. A fund that determines a timeline, then invests in conservative stocks during the early years and aggressive stocks during the later years.
    b. A fund that determines a timeline, then invests in aggressive stocks during the early years and conservative stocks during the later years.
    c. A fund that chooses a target date, and then begins investing on that date.
    d. A fund that is automatically cashed out on the target date.

3. This is a fee charged for active management of a mutual fund.
    a. Back-end load
    b. Front-end load
    c. Expense ratio
    d. Load fee

4. All mutual funds are actively managed.
    a. True
    b. False

5. What is the main difference between a mutual fund and an ETF?
    a. A mutual fund has fees; ETFs don't.

b. Mutual funds are passively managed; ETFs are actively managed.
c. Mutual funds can be traded once a day; ETFs can be traded throughout the day.
d. Mutual funds are curated by Mr. Fuzzy Nuts; ETFs are curated by computers.

6. How are mutual fund earnings divided among fund owners?
   a. Proportionally; more money to people who own more shares, less money to people who own fewer shares
   b. Evenly; total earnings are divided by the number of investors and distributed
   c. In order according to date of purchase.
   d. Annually

7. How should you invest for retirement?
   a. Target-based funds
   b. Low fee index funds
   c. High risk stocks
   d. Any dang way you want, provided you understand what you are investing in

8. What is the purpose of rebalancing a portfolio?
   a. To increase earnings
   b. To keep the fund in the best position to reach its goal
   c. To increase earnings and avoid losses
   d. To find the perfect balance

9. Why do managed funds have fees?
   a. To pay the manager and other administrative costs
   b. To pay for insider tips that allow the fund to earn more
   c. To keep the fund out of the reach of the average investor
   d. To compensate managers for earning better-than-market returns

10. The benefit of stock picking is that it gets higher returns than index funds do.

    a. True
    b. False

11. What is the "magic" of mutual funds? Pick the best answer.

    a. It allows investors to pick stocks like the professionals.
    b. It allows investors to purchase shares of stock in different sectors.
    c. It allows investors to purchase high-priced stocks.
    d. It allows investors to own a stake in many different companies by purchasing a single share.

12. Passive investing is free.

    a. True
    b. False

13. You need a full-service broker to purchase an ETF.

    a. True
    b. False

14. Why is Business Kitty cynical?

    a. He thinks that fund managers don't really know what they're doing.
    b. He thinks fund managers lack the ability to pick good stocks for mutual funds.
    c. He thinks fund managers don't have a compelling reason to pick good stocks for the funds that they manage.
    d. He thinks fund managers charge too much for their services.

15. Is it possible to change a complete A-hole?

    a. Yes, with patience and love.
    b. Possibly, but only if the A-hole *wants* to change.

c. Unlikely, unless the A-hole experiences some sort of traumatic event that makes him reevaluate his life.
d. Maybe, but why bother?

Answer Key to Quiz 4

1. A

   This is why people are so excited about index funds. Low fees.

2. B

   Early year risk/later year safety is the way the game is usually played. (That doesn't mean you *have* to do it that way, though.)

3. C

   The management fees are paid for with the expense ratio. (But fund owners may encounter those other fees as well.)

4. B

   For example, an index fund is a kind of mutual fund, and they aren't actively managed.

5. C

   It's a trader thing.

6. A

   It's a fair system—the more you pay into the fund, the more money you can make when it earns profits.

7. D

   It's all about you, baby.

8. B

   The result of rebalancing might be more earnings, but the purpose of rebalancing is to keep the fund on track with a future goal.

9. A

   "A" is the best answer, because the fees don't *only* go to the manager of the fund. Those fees can be spent on other things as well.

10. B

    There is no way to predict returns.

11. D

    Choices"A," "B," and "C" could all be correct as well, but choice "D" gives the best answer.

12. B

    It has low fees, but it's not free. Don't you remember the "Ain't Nothin' Free, Baby" chapter?

13. B

    Nope—you can buy it just like any other share of stock.

14. C

    He probably believes all the other stuff too, but answer "C" is the precise reason for his cynicism.

15. I've tried answering this one for people and I have gotten nowhere. Nobody listens. You're going to do what you want to do anyway, so just leave me out of it.

Congratulations! If you were able to ace this last quiz, then your Mojo cup runneth over. As you'll see on the next page, you have come a long way from Market Newbie status. Read on and bask in the glory of your accomplishments.

Closing

Now that you have come to the end of the book, you may be experiencing a range of emotions—pride, euphoria, bemused resignation . . . (But not dizziness. If you're feeling dizzy, go back and check into that tick fever thing.) And while the end of an enjoyable journey can be bittersweet, the "sweet" part can be found in reflecting on how far you have come.

Even though this book is an *introduction* to the stock market, finishing it provides you with a veritable treasure trove of valuable knowledge that you can start drawing from right away. Because I did my best to make this less of a textbook and more of an "informational romp," you may not even be aware of *just how much* information you have absorbed up to this point. Think about it:

You understand essential market vocabulary.

Even casual conversations about finance and/or basic texts about the stock market contain specialized terminology that can catch you off guard and make it harder for you to make sense of new information. Having a good working knowledge of investing vocabulary and concepts (i.e. expense ratios, index funds, passive investing) will give you confidence to continue reading, learning, and exploring the world of finance.

You understand that risk is an inherent part of investing.

You aren't going to fall for any get-rich-quick schemes. You know that all investments bring some kind of risk with them and that there are no guarantees in the market. Furthermore, you understand the unique relationship between risk and return—that is, when you increase your possibilities for earning, you increase your exposure to risk. Conversely, when you reduce your risk, you also reduce your earning potential. (When there is finally a low-risk/high-reward investment out there, I will be sure to let you know about it.) Understanding the nature of risk in the stock market will help you make informed decisions about how to earn profits while protecting your investment.

You understand the role that diversification plays in your portfolio.
When you start building your portfolio, you will have an overarching vision for its composition. Being aware of the need to diversify your holdings means that you will consider companies that represent different sectors of the economy, as well as companies of different sizes (large cap, mid cap, and small cap). Because you know about different investing options, you can purchase shares of specific companies through stock picking, or you can buy into multiple companies at once through mutual funds, index funds or ETFs. (Or even better, you can treat those options as offerings at a salad bar—picking and choosing as you see fit to create your perfect mix.)

You understand the importance of determining a personal investment plan.
Knowing there is no such thing as a "one-size-fits-all" portfolio, you are confident enough to assess your financial goals, consider your risk capacity and risk tolerance, and determine a level of diversification that suits you. Using that information, you can be certain that your investment is 100 percent tailored to your objectives. Rather than blindly following suggested stock market advice or throwing darts and feces around like Mr. Fuzzy Nuts, you can create a personalized investment vehicle and understand exactly how its different components work together to build wealth for you.

Now that you can lay claim to these significant accomplishments, I have no other choice but to boot you out of the nest and encourage you to fly. Fly! Fly into the sunset proud and free, with the gentle strains of 70s soft rock serving as the soundtrack for your journey. As you go on your way, I hope you remember the jolly good times we had together. Far beyond just learning the basics of the stock market, we had a multi-sensory experience, mixing diverse elements like hard-core number crunching (amaze your friends by using the Dow Divisor) with infusions of pure whimsy (Weren't Mr. Fuzzy Nuts and Business Kitty a hoot?). I do hope you enjoyed it. But even more than that, I hope you found it useful.

Now that the educational component is behind you, it's time to get down to business. Go get yourself a double shot Loggins Latte and put your Market Mojo to work.

BIBLIOGRAPHY

About the SEC. (n.d.). Retrieved July 30, 2017 from https://www.sec.gov/about.shtml.

All, K. (2012, January 10). Investing 101: The difference between stocks and ETFs. Retrieved July 31, 2017 from https://www.fool.com/investing/general/2012/01/10/investing-101-the-difference-between-stocks-and-et.aspx.

Amadeo, K. (2017, June 29). The S&P 500 and how it works. Retrieved July 31, 2017 from https://www.thebalance.com/what-is-the-sandp-500-3305888.

Amazon.com, Inc. common stock quote & summary data. (2017, July 28). Retrieved August 1, 2017 from http://www.nasdaq.com/symbol/amzn.

Animal collective nouns. (n.d.). Retrieved July 31, 2017 from http://www.thealmightyguru.com/Pointless/AnimalGroups.html.

Annual report. (n.d.). Retrieved July 30, 2017 from http://www.investopedia.com/terms/a/annualreport.asp.

Appreciation. (n.d.). Retrieved July 30, 2017 from http://www.investopedia.com/terms/a/appreciation.asp.

B, Sneaky. (2004, January 24). Scrilla. Retrieved July 31, 2017 from http://www.urbandictionary.com/define.php?term=scrilla.

Balakrishnan, A. (2017, May 8). Apple market cap tops $800 billion for the first time. Retrieved July 31, 2017 from https://www.cnbc.com/2017/05/08/apple-market-capitalization-hits-800-billion.html.

Beginner's guide to asset allocation, diversification and rebalancing. (n.d.). Retrieved July 31, 2017 from https://investor.gov/additional-resources/general-resources/publications-research/info-sheets/beginners'-guide-asset.

Berger, R. (2017, March 27). An S&P 500 index fund—is it a good investment? Retrieved July 31, 2017 from https://www.forbes.com/sites/robertberger/2017/03/27/an-sp-500-index-fund-is-it-a-good-investment/#462193fe73b2.

Biggest stock exchanges in the world. (n.d.). Retrieved July 30, 2017 from http://www.worldatlas.com/articles/biggest-stock-exchanges-in-the-world.html.

Blue chip (stock market). (n.d.). Retrieved July 31, 2017 from https://en.wikipedia.org/wiki/Blue_chip_(stock_market).

Brokers and online trading: full service or discount? (n.d.). Retrieved July 31, 2017 from http://www.investopedia.com/university/broker/broker2.asp.

Calculating the Dow. (n.d.). Retrieved July 31, 2017 from http://news.morningstar.com/classroom2/course.asp?docId=2958&page=2.

Carther, S. (2017, April 21). Socially responsible mutual funds. Retrieved July 31, 2017 from http://www.investopedia.com/articles/mutualfund/03/030503.asp.

Carther, S. (2017, April 26). Socially (ir)responsible mutual funds. Retrieved July 31, 2017 from http://www.investopedia.com/articles/mutualfund/03/031903.asp.

Corkery, M. (2009, August 21). What would Charles Dow and Edward Jones think? Retrieved July 31, 2017 from https://blogs.wsj.com/deals/2009/08/21/what-would-charles-dow-and-edward-jones-think/.

Definition of 'Dow Divisor.' (n.d.). Retrieved July 31, 2017 from http://www.investopedia.com/terms/d/dowdivisor.asp.

Desjardins, J. (2017, April 11). Here are the 20 biggest stock exchanges in the world. Retrieved July 30, 2017 http://uk.businessinsider.com/here-are-the-20-biggest-stock-exchanges-in-the-world-2017-4?IR=T.

Difference between the two largest stock exchanges in the U.S. (2013, August 5). Retrieved July 30, 2017 from http://www.internationalfinancemagazine.com/article/Difference-Between-the-Two-Largest-Stock-Exchanges-in-the-US.html.

Difference between stock market and stock exchange. (2015, September 1). Retrieved July 30, 2017 from http://researchpedia.info/difference-between-stock-market-and-stock-exchange/.

DiLallo, M., R. Duprey & D. Miller (2017, June 5). Should you buy into the hype surrounding these stocks? Retrieved July 30, 2017 from https://www.fool.com/investing/2017/06/05/should-you-buy-into-the-hype-surrounding-these-sto.aspx.

Dodd-Frank Act. (n.d.). Retrieved July 31, 2017 from http://www.cftc.gov/LawRegulation/DoddFrankAct/index.htm.

Dow Jones Transportation Average—DJTA. (n.d.). Retrieved July 31, 2017 from http://www.investopedia.com/terms/d/djta.asp.

Dow Jones Industrial Average—DJIA. (n.d.). Retrieved July 31, 2017 from http://www.investopedia.com/terms/d/djia.asp.

Dow Jones Industrial Average—Divisor History. (n.d.). Retrieved July 31, 2017 from http://siblisresearch.com/data/dow-jones-divisor-history/.

Egan, M. (2015, June 9). Jack Ma wishes Alibaba never went public. Retrieved August 1, 2017 from http://money.cnn.com/2015/06/09/investing/jack-ma-alibaba-ipo-china/index.html.

Exchange-traded fund. (n.d.). Retrieved July 31, 2017 from http://www.investopedia.com/terms/e/etf.asp.

Expense ratio. (n.d.). Retrieved July 31, 2017 from http://www.morningstar.com/InvGlossary/expense_ratio.aspx.

Fast answers: annual report. (n.d.). Retrieved July 30, 2017 from https://www.sec.gov/fast-answers/answers-annrephtm.html.

Fedorov, S. (n.d.). Dividend payment factors. Retrieved July 30, 2017 from http://thefinancebase.com/dividend-payment-factors-2470.html.

Fontinelle, A. (2017, May 31). Why do some companies pay a dividend, while other companies do not? Retrieved July 30, 2017 from http://www.investopedia.com/ask/answers/12/why-do-some-companies-pay-a-dividend.asp.

Forms list. (n.d.). Retrieved July 30, 2017 from https://www.sec.gov/forms.

Full-service broker. (n.d.). Retrieved July 31, 2017 from http://www.investopedia.com/terms/f/fullservicebroker.asp.

Fund Manager. (n.d.). Retrieved July 31, 2017 from http://www.investopedia.com/terms/f/fundmanager.asp.

Grammar: indexes vs. indices. (2006, September 28). Retrieved July 31, 2017 from https://federalist.wordpress.com/2006/09/28/grammar-indexes-vs-indices/.

Grimms' Fairy Tales. (n.d.). Retrieved July 31, 2017 from http://www.grimmstories.com/language.php?grimm=187&l=en&r=de.

Guide to stock picking strategies. (n.d.). Retrieved July 31, 2017 from http://www.investopedia.com/university/stockpicking/.

Henry Varnum Poor. (n.d.). Retrieved July 31, 2017 from https://en.wikipedia.org/wiki/Henry_Varnum_Poor.

Hoffman, D. (2016, March 31). What stock-market return should your financial plan assume? Retrieved August 1, 2017 from https://blogs.wsj.com/experts/2016/03/31/what-stock-market-return-should-your-financial-plan-assume/.

Hoffman, G. (2017, April 28). Here's how rich you would be if you invested in Amazon at its IPO. Retrieved July 31, 2017 from https://finance.yahoo.com/news/heres-rich-invested-amazon-ipo-191000358.html.

Horton, M. (2015, April 20). What rights do all common shareholders have? Retrieved July 30, 2017 from http://www.investopedia.com/ask/answers/042015/what-rights-do-all-common-shareholders-have.asp.

How are indexes weighted? (n.d.). Retrieved July 31, 2017 from http://www.ftserussell.com/research-insights/education-center/how-are-indexes-weighted.

How to calculate price-weighted average for stocks. (n.d.). Retrieved July 31, 2017 from https://www.fool.com/knowledge-center/how-to-calculate-price-weighted-average-for-stocks.aspx.

Hulbert, M. (2017, May 13). This is how many fund managers actually beat index funds. Retrieved July 31, 2017 from http://www.marketwatch.com/story/why-way-fewer-actively-managed-funds-beat-the-sp-than-we-thought-2017-04-24.

Hunkar, D. (2010, May 18). Top 25 Nasdaq stocks ranked by market cap. Retrieved July 30, 2017 from https://seekingalpha.com/article/194270-top-25-nasdaq-stocks-ranked-by-market-cap.

Kerr, D. (2013, November 7). Pets.com gives a blast from the dot bomb past. Retrieved August 1, 2017 from https://www.cnet.com/news/pets-com-gives-a-blast-from-the-dot-bomb-past/.

Kilgore, T. (2015, December 24). Dow divisor change gives its stock a little more influence. Retrieved July 31, 2017 from http://www.marketwatch.com/story/dow-divisor-change-gives-its-stocks-a-little-more-influence-2015-12-24.

Languages of Papua New Guinea. (n.d.). Retrieved July 31, 2017 from https://en.wikipedia.org/wiki/Languages_of_Papua_New_Guinea.

List: access capital. (n.d.) Retrieved August 1, 2017 from http://business.nasdaq.com/list.

List of S&P 500 companies. (n.d.). Retrieved July 31, 2017 from https://en.wikipedia.org/wiki/List_of_S%26P_500_companies.

List of stock exchanges. (n.d.). Retrieved from http://www.wikinvest.com/wiki/List_of_Stock_Exchanges.

Load Funds. (2014, September 23). Retrieved from http://mutualfunds.com/load-funds/.

Loan Calculator. (n.d.). Retrieved July 30, 2017, from http://www.bankrate.com/calculators/mortgages/loan-calculator.aspx?loanAmount=100000&years=10.000&terms=120&interestRate=3.000&loanStartDate=30%2BJul%2B2017&email=&lightbox=true&show=false&showRt=true&prods=393&monthlyAdditionalAmount=0&yearlyAdditionalAmount=0&yearlyPaymentMonth=%2BJul%2B&oneTimeAdditionalPayment=0&oneTimeAdditionalPaymentInMY=%2BAug%2B2017&ic_id=mtg_loan_calc_calculate_btn.

Loan Calculator. (n.d.) Retrieved July 30, 2017, from http://www.calculator.net/loan-calculator.html?cloanamount=100000&cloanterm=5&cloantermmonth=0&cinterestrate=3&ccompound=monthly&cpayback=month&x=46&y=15.

Mac, R. (2014, September 22). Alibaba claims title for largest global IPO ever with extra share sales. Retrieved July 31, 2017 from https://www.forbes.com/sites/ryanmac/2014/09/22/alibaba-claims-title-for-largest-global-ipo-ever-with-extra-share-sales/.

Mack, A. (2015, October 26). The long-beaked echidna: can we save the earth's oldest living mammal? Retrieved July 31, 2017 from https://news.mongabay.com/2015/10/the-long-beaked-echidna-can-we-save-the-earths-oldest-living-mammal/.

Market capitalization defined. (2017, June 7). Retrieved July 31, 2017 from http://www.investopedia.com/articles/basics/03/031703.asp.

Morah, C. (n.d.). What are all of the securities markets in the U.S.A.? Retrieved July 30, 2017 from http://www.investopedia.com/ask/answers/08/security-market-usa.asp.

Murray, J. (2016, August 6). Public Company vs. Private Company—What's the Difference? Retrieved July 30, 2017 from https://www.thebalance.com/public-company-vs-private-company-what-s-the-difference-398422.

Nasdaq. (n.d.). Retrieved July 31, 2017 from http://www.investopedia.com/terms/n/nasdaq.asp.

NASDAQ. (n.d.). Retrieved July 30, 2017 from https://en.wikipedia.org/wiki/NASDAQ.

NASDAQ composite index methodology. (n.d.). Retrieved July 31, 2017 from https://indexes.nasdaqomx.com/docs/methodology_COMP.pdf.

NASDAQ's story. (n.d.). Retrieved August 1, 2017 from http://business.nasdaq.com/discover/nasdaq-story.

NASDAQ vs. NYSE. (n.d.). Retrieved July 30, 2017 from http://www.investorguide.com/article/15710/nasdaq-vs-nyse-d1412/

Nas-T, Funk. The Man. (2003, August 11). Retrieved July 31, 2017 from http://www.urbandictionary.com/define.php?term=The%20Man.

Nazar, J. (2013, September 6). The 10 best and worst IPOs: where are they now? Retrieved July 31, 2017 from http://www.businessinsider.com/the-10-best-and-worst-ipos-2013-12?IR=T.

New York Stock Exchange. (n.d.). Retrieved August 1, 2017 from http://www.u-s-history.com/pages/h1806.html.

New York Stock Exchange. (n.d.). Retrieved August 1, 2017 from https://en.wikipedia.org/wiki/New_York_Stock_Exchange.

New York Stock Exchange: a timeline. (2011, February 15). Retrieved August 1, 2017 from https://usatoday30.usatoday.com/money/industries/brokerage/2011-02-15-nyse-timeline_N.htm.

New York Stock Exchange—company listings. (n.d.). Retrieved August 1, 2017 from http://www.advfn.com/nyse/newyorkstockexchange.asp.

New York Stock Exchange—NYSE. (n.d.). Retrieved July 30, 2017 from http://www.investopedia.com/terms/n/nyse.asp.

Osbon, M. (2016, December 12). How to figure out your investment timeline. Retrieved July 31, 2017 from http://www.investopedia.com/advisor-network/articles/121216/how-figure-out-your-investment-timeline/.

Pablo Cruise: Music. (n.d.). Retrieved July 30, 2017 from https://www.pablocruise.com/about.

Paypal holding market cap history (PYPL). (n.d.). Retrieved July 31, 2017 from http://www.macrotrends.net/stocks/charts/PYPL/market-cap/paypal-market-cap-history.

Price-weighted index. (n.d.). Retrieved July 31, 2017 from http://www.investopedia.com/terms/p/priceweightedindex.asp.

Public vs. private companies: how do they differ? (n.d.). Retrieved July 30, 2017 from https://www.allbusiness.com/public-vs-private-companies-how-do-they-differ-2304-1.html.

Pump and dump. (n.d.). Retrieved July 30, 2017 from http://www.investopedia.com/terms/p/pumpanddump.asp.

Research before you invest. (n.d.). Retrieved July 30, 2017 from https://www.investor.gov/research-before-you-invest.

Roos, D. (n.d.). 10 Biggest IPO flops in history. Retrieved July 31, 2017 from http://money.howstuffworks.com/10-biggest-ipo-flops4.htm.

Roy, T. (2017, May 17). Coca-Cola: Warren Buffet's favorite stock. Retrieved July 30, 2017 from http://www.dividend.com/news/2017/05/17/coca-cola-warren-buffett-favoritestock/.

Sanford, J. (2014, June 19). Confessions of a financial advisor. Retrieved July 31, 2017 from https://www.cnbc.com/2014/06/19/confessions-of-a-financial-advisorpersonal-financecommentary.html.

Securities and Exchange Commission. (n.d.). Retrieved July 30, 2017 from http://www.history.com/topics/securities-and-exchange-commission.

Seth, Shobhit. (n.d.). What The Dow Means and Why We Calculate it the Way We Do. Retrieved July 31, 2017 from http://www.investopedia.com/articles/investing/082714/what-dow-means-and-why-we-calculate-it-way-we-do.asp.

Shareholder Rights. (n.d.). Retrieved July 30, 2017 from https://corporations.uslegal.com/shareholder-rights/.

Sparks, D. (2016, August 10). Apple's Stock Split History. Retrieved July 31, 2017 from https://www.fool.com/investing/2016/08/10/apples-stock-split-history.aspx.

SPIVA U.S. Scorecard. (2017). Retrieved August 1, 2017 from https://us.spindices.com/documents/spiva/spiva-us-year-end-2016.pdf.

Stein, C. (2017, July 6). Active vs. Passive Investing. Retrieved July 31, 2017 from https://www.bloomberg.com/quicktake/active-vs-passive-investing.

Stein, C. (2016 September 22). The professor who was right about index funds all along. Retrieved July 31, 2017 from https://www.bloomberg.com/news/articles/2016-09-22/the-professor-who-was-right-about-index-funds-all-along.

Stock split. (n.d.). Retrieved July 31, 2017 from http://www.investopedia.com/terms/s/stocksplit.asp.

The 30 Dow Jones Stocks. (2015, May 18). Retrieved July 31, 2017 from https://www.fool.com/investing/general/2015/05/18/the-30-dow-jones-stocks.aspx.

The importance of diversification. (2016, July 1). Retrieved July 31, 2017 from http://www.investopedia.com/articles/02/111502.asp.

The NYSE and Nasdaq: how they work. (2017, April 28). Retrieved July 30, 2017 from http://www.investopedia.com/articles/basics/03/103103.asp.

T. Rowe Price Group, Inc. (TROW). (2017, July 28). Retrieved July 31, 2017 from https://finance.yahoo.com/quote/TROW/.

Understanding stock splits. (2017, March 6). Retrieved July 31, 2017 from http://www.investopedia.com/articles/01/072501.asp.

What are key factors that influence dividend policies? (n.d.). Retrieved July 30, 2017, from https://www.fool.com/knowledge-center/key-factors-that-influence-dividend-policies.aspx.

What are mutual funds? (n.d.). Retrieved July 31, 2017 from https://www.fidelity.com/learning-center/investment-products/mutual-funds/what-are-mutual-funds.

What is a stock index? (n.d.). Retrieved July 31, 2017 from https://www.fool.com/knowledge-center/what-is-a-stock-index.aspx.

What is the difference between investing and trading? (n.d.). Retrieved July 31, 2017 from http://www.investopedia.com/ask/answers/12/difference-investing-trading.asp.

What's the difference between publicly- and privately-held companies? (2017, May 10). Retrieved July 30, 2017 from http://www.investopedia.com/ask/answers/162.asp.

What's wrong with full-service brokers? (n.d.). Retrieved July 31, 2017 from https://www.fool.com/investing/brokerage/whats-wrong-with-full-service-brokers.aspx.

Williams, J. (2017, October 7). The indexing effect: does inclusion in an index increase the price of a stock? Retrieved September 2, 2017 from https://www.wealthdaily.com/articles/the-indexing-effect/8369.

Photo Credits

1.1 Mills, K.G. (Artist). (2017, July 28). *Kathy's Accordion Café* [digital file]. (Kathy G. Mills Collection).

1.2 Pekárková, V. (Owner). (n.d.). *Café Imperial Prague* [digital file]. Retrieved from http://www.cafeimperial.cz. Reprinted with permission.

1.3 Mills, K.G. (Artist). (2017, July 28). *Stock Market Magic* [altered digital file]. (Kathy G. Mills Collection) Original image retrieved from Pixabay https://pixabay.com/en/magic-wand-magician-magic-trick-1081149/.

1.4 Mills, K.G. (Artist). (2017, July 28). *Dividends* [altered digital file]. (Kathy G. Mills Collection) Original images retrieved from Pixabay https://pixabay.com/en/man-person-money-big-fifties-bag-304616/ https://pixabay.com/en/black-black-white-dollar-sign-2029505/.

1.5 Mills, K.G. (Artist). (2017, July 28). *Buying Stock in Apple 1976, Cashing in 2017* [altered digital files]. (Kathy G. Mills Collection) Original images retrieved from Pixabay https://pixabay.com/en/business-stick-people-handshake-2323757/ and https://pixabay.com/en/money-euro-profit-currency-1015277/ .

1.6 Mills, K.G. (Artist). (2017, July 28). *Stock Market God* [altered digital file]. (Kathy G. Mills Collection) Original image retrieved from Pixabay https: https://pixabay.com/en/profit-success-graph-3d-rendering-2395780/.

1.7 Mills, K.G. (Artist). (2017, July 28). *Well, poop* [altered digital files]. (Kathy G. Mills Collection) Original images retrieved from Pixabay https://pixabay.com/en/down-arrow-red-pointing-downward-24813/ and https://pixabay.com/en/males-3d-model-isolated-3d-model-2322821/.

2.1 Vašek, J. (Photographer). (2014, October 11). *Croissants* [digital file]. Retrieved from Pixabay https://pixabay.com/en/croissants-jelly-breakfast-569075/.

3.1 *United States Securities and Exchange Commission Official Seal* (n.d.).[digital file]. Retrieved from Wikimedia Commons https://commons.wikimedia.org/wiki/File:Seal_of_the_United_States_Securities_and_Exchange_Commission.jpg. Public Domain.

3.2 Mills, K.G. (Artist). (2017, July 28). *Dear SEC* [digital file]. (Kathy G. Mills Collection).

4.1 TomasEEE (Photographer). (2012, March 13). *The New York Stock Exchange* [digital file]. Retrieved from Wikimedia Commons https://commons.wikimedia.org/wiki/File:New_York_Stock_Exchange_-_panoramio_(2).jpg. Distributed under the Creative Commons Attribution 3.0 Unported license.

4.2 Notari, T. (Photographer). (2005, June 20). *Nasdaq* [digital file]. Retrieved from Wikimedia Commons https://commons.wikimedia.org/wiki/File:Nasdaq_5.jpg. Distributed under the Creative Commons Attribution-Share Alike 2.0 Generic license.

4.3 George, A. (Photographer). (2011, September 23). *Richard Simmons Attending the AARP's 2011 Life@50+ National Event and Expo in September 2011* [digital file]. Retrieved from Wikimedia Commons https://commons.wikimedia.org/wiki/File:RichardSimmonsSept2011.jpg.

Distributed under the Creative Commons Attribution-Share Alike 3.0 Unported license.

Guilane (Artist). (n.d.). *Two Question Marks* [digital file]. Retrieved from Pixabay https://pixabay.com/en/question-mark-question-mark-423604/.

Watanabe, K. (Photographer). (2007, August 16). *Diet Coke Can* [digital file]. Retrieved from Wikimedia Commons https://commons.wikimedia.org/wiki/File:Diet_Coke_can_US_1982.jpg. Public Domain.

5.1 Bøtter, J. (Photographer). (2006, February 13). *The Pets.com sock puppet* [digital file]. Originally posted on Flickr https://www.flickr.com/photos/jakecaptive/99410167/ and retrieved from Wikimedia Commons https://commons.wikimedia.org/wiki/File:Pets.com_sockpuppet.jpg. Distributed under the Creative Commons Attribution 2.0 Generic License.

6.1 Underwood & Underwood (Photographers). (1937, March). *Amelia Earhart Standing Under Nose of her Lockheed Model 10-E Electra* [digital file]. (National Portrait Gallery, Smithsonian Institution). Retrieved from Wikimedia Commons https://commons.wikimedia.org/wiki/File:Amelia_Earhart_standing_under_nose_of_her_Lockheed_Model_10-E_Electra,_small.jpg . Public Domain

6.2 Free-Photos (Owner). (n.d.). *Writing, Pen* [digital file]. Retrieved from Pixabay https://pixabay.com/en/writing-pen-man-boy-male-ink-1149962/.

7.1 *Charles Dow.* (n.d.). [digital file]. Retrieved from Wikimedia Commons https://commons.wikimedia.org/wiki/File:Charles_Henry_Dow.jpg. Public domain.

7.2 Mills, K.G. (Artist). (2017, September 1). *Dow Sectors.* [digital file]. (Kathy G. Mills Collection).

7.3 Higgins, R. (Photographer). (n.d.). *Confused Woman* [digital file]. Retrieved from Pixabay https://pixabay.com/en/confused-woman-doubt-female-girl-2385799/.

7.4 TukTuk Design (Artist). (n.d.) *Smiley* [digital file]. Retrieved from Pixabay https://pixabay.com/en/smiley-emoticon-happy-face-icon-1635449/.

7.5 Rockefeller, J.D. (Owner). (1887). *Standard Oil Company Stock Certificate* [digital file]. Retrieved from Wikimedia Commons https://commons.wikimedia.org/wiki/File:Acción_de_la_Standard_Oil.png. Public domain.

7.6 TukTuk Design (Artist). (n.d.). *Smiley, Emoticon* [digital file]. Retrieved from Pixabay https://pixabay.com/en/smiley-emoticon-happy-face-icon-1635448/.

7.7 TukTuk Design (Artist). (n.d.). *Smiley, Emoticon, Money* [digital file]. Retrieved from Pixabay https://pixabay.com/en/smiley-emoticon-money-dollars-rich-1635465/.

7.8 *Dow Jones Industrial Average.* (2017). [digital file]. Retrieved from https://www.globalfinancialdata.com/gfdblog/?p=1426.

7.9 Mills, K.G. (Artist). (2017, July 25). *Secret Meaning in the Dow Chart.* [altered digital file]. Original file retrieved from https://www.globalfinancialdata.com/gfdblog/?p=1426.

8.1 Snippets101 (Artist). (2008, July 18). *Statler and Waldorf* [digital file]. Retrieved from Flickr https://www.flickr.com/photos/snippets101/2686592689. Distributed under the Creative Commons Attribution-NoDerivs 2.0 Generic license.

8.2 Sasint (Photographer). (n.d.). *Adult Amorous Asia* [digital file]. Retrieved from Pixabay https://pixabay.com/en/adult-amorous-asia-girlfriend-1807617/.

8.3 Mills, K.G. (Artist). (2017, July 27). *S&P Allocation Chart* [digital file]. (Kathy G. Mills Collection).

8.4 *S&P 500 Index from 1950 to 2016.* (2017). [digital file]. Retrieved from Wikipedia https://en.wikipedia.org/wiki/S%26P_500_Index.

8.5 Mills, K.G. (Artist). (2017, July 31). *Secret Meaning in the S&P 500 Index from 1950 to 2016.* [altered digital file]. Original file retrieved from https://en.wikipedia.org/wiki/S%26P_500_Index.

9.1 Naz-T, Funk. The Man. (2013). Retrieved from The Urban Dictionary http://www.urbandictionary.com/define.php?term=The+Man&utm_source=search-action.

9.2 *NASDAQ Composite History Chart March 1, 1971 Through December 30, 2016.* (2017). [digital file]. Retrieved from http://www.fedprimerate.com/nasdaq-composite-history-chart.htm.

9.3 *Henry VIII Revealed in the NASDAQ Composite History Chart 1971-2016.* (2017, July 31). [altered digital file]. Original file retrieved from http://www.fedprimerate.com/nasdaq-composite-history-chart.htm.

10.1 Mojpe (Photographer). (n.d.). *Woman, Blow, Blowing* [digital file]. Retrieved from Pixabay https://pixabay.com/en/woman-blow-blowing-nose-hand-chief-698953/.

10.2 Marceau, T. (Photographer). (1903). *William Kissam Vanderbilt II* [altered digital file]. Original image retrieved from Wikimedia Commons https://commons.wikimedia.org/wiki/File:William_K_Vanderbilt_IIc.jpg. Public domain.

10.3 FreeStockPhotos.biz (Owner). (n.d.). *A teen girl texting while driving* [altered digital file]. Original image retrieved from FreeStockPhotos http://www.freestockphotos.biz/stockphoto/15862. Public domain.

10.4 CNX Open Stax (Owner). (2016, January 22). *Lyme Rash* [digital file]. Retrieved from Wikimedia Commons https://commons.wikimedia.org/wiki/File:OSC_Microbio_12_02_LymeRash.jpg. Distributed under the Creative Commons Attribution 4.0 International license.

11.1 Mills, K.G. (Artist). (2017, July 31). *Are You an Investor or a Trader?* [altered digital file]. Original file retrieved from http://americanhistory.si.edu/collections/search/main?edan_q=&edan_fq[]=set_name:%22Smithsonian+Libraries+Trade+Literature+Collections%22&custom_search_id=collections-search. (The National Museum of American History Trade Catalog Collection). Public domain.

11.2 Proszek, T. (Photographer). (n.d.). *Hedgehog* [digital file]. Retrieved from Pixabay https://pixabay.com/en/hedgehog-spring-animal-548335/.

11.3 jtkerb (Photographer). (2008, March 12). *Ethiopian Highland Hare* [digital file]. Retrieved from Wikimedia Commons https://commons.wikimedia.org/wiki/File:Ethiopian_Highland_Hare_(Lepus_starcki)_running.jpg. Distributed under the Creative Commons Attribution 2.0 Generic license.

12.1 Levchenko, S. (Photographer). (n.d.). *Balloons for Party* [digital file]. Retrieved from Unsplash https://unsplash.com/search/blueballoons?photo=Meeycb5dpXs.

12.2 Geralt. (Photographer). (n.d.). *Despair Alone* [digital file]. Retrieved from Pixabay https://pixabay.com/en/despair-alone-being-alone-archetype-513529/.

12.3 Mills, K.G. (Photographer). (2017, July 28). *Sheriff Kathy* [digital file]. (Kathy G. Mills Collection).

12.4 Mills, K.G. (Artist). (2017, July 29). *Risk, Earnings, Losses* [digital file]. (Kathy G. Mills Collection).

13.1 Whittome, A. (Photographer). (2005, January 31). *Echidna Tachyglossus aculeatus* [digital file]. Retrieved from Wikimedia Commons https://commons.wikimedia.org/wiki/File:Echinda_burningwell.jpg. Public Domain.

13.2 Amaya, Bea (Photographer). (n.d.). *Rabaul Papua New Guinea* [digital file]. Retrieved from Pixabay https://pixabay.com/en/rabaul-papua-new-guinea-travel-2267366/.

13.3 dMz (Photographer). (n.d.). *Crocodile* [digital file]. Retrieved from Pixabay https://pixabay.com/en/crocodile-reptile-dangerous-2293232/.

14.1 Travelwayoflife (Photographer). (2011, May 24). *Five Burrowing Owls* [altered digital file]. Original image retrieved from Wikimedia Commons https://commons.wikimedia.org/wiki/File:Athene_cunicularia_20110524_02.jpg. Distributed under the Creative Commons Attribution-Share Alike 2.0 Generic.

14.2 *Forrester Kangaroo Mob.* (n.d.). [altered digital file]. Original image retrieved from Wikipedia https://en.wikipedia.org/wiki/File:Forrester-Kangaroo-mob.jpg. Distributed under the Creative Commons Attribution-Share Alike 3.0 license.

14.3 Dilmen, N. (Photographer). (n.d.). *Wildebeest Connochaetes taurinus* [altered digital file] Original image retrieved from Wikimedia Commons https://commons.wikimedia.org/wiki/File:Wildebeest_Connochaetes_taurinus_in_Tanzania_4246_Nevit.jpg. Distributed under the Creative Commons Attribution-Share Alike 3.0 Unported license.

14.4 Seto, D. (Photographer). (2008, November 11). *WWE Wrestler Triple H at a Live Event on WWE Friday Night SmackDown* [digital file]. Retrieved from Wikimedia Commons https://commons.wikimedia.org/wiki/File:Triple_H_WWE_Champion_2008.jpg. Distributed under the Creative Commons Attribution-Share Alike 3.0 Unported license.

15.1 Lottery Post (Owner). (2008). *Britain's First Nudist Lottery Winners* [digital image]. Retrieved from https://www.lotterypost.com/news/178433. Reprinted with permission.

15.2 Open Clip-Art Vectors (Owner). (n.d.). *Angel Devil Female* [altered digital file.] Original image retrieved from Pixabay https://pixabay.com/en/angel-devil-female-guardian-human-1296384/.

15.3 Mills, K.G. (Artist). (August 1, 2017). *Business Kitty is Skeptical* [altered digital file]. Original file retrieved from https://pixabay.com/en/cat-laptop-pet-animal-244060/.

16.1 Midori, S. (Photographer). (2006, November 14). *M. fascicularis* [digital file]. Retrieved from Wikimedia Commons https://commons.wikimedia.org/wiki/Macaca#/media/File:Ngarai_Sianok_s

umatran_monkey.jpg. Distributed under the CC-BY-SA-2.0 and GFDL licenses.

17.1 Stephens, Justin. (Photographer). (2008, October 6). *Hugh Laurie 2* [digital file]. Retrieved from Flickr on July 30, 2017 https://www.flickr.com/photos/buou/2919265162/in/photostream/. Distributed under the Attribution-ShareAlike 2.0 Generic license.

17.2 Mills, K.G. (Artist). (2017, July 30). *Sally's Chart at 20* [digital file]. (Kathy G. Mills collection)

17.3 Mills, K.G. (Artist). (2017, July 30). *Sally's Chart at 40* [digital file]. (Kathy G. Mills collection)

17.4 Mills, K.G. (Artist). (2017, July 30). *Sally's Chart at 60* [digital file]. (Kathy G. Mills collection)

17.5 Mills, K.G. (Artist). (2017, July 30). *No Time-Share in Dhaka* [altered digital file]. Original image retrieved from Pixabay https://pixabay.com/en/dollar-currency-capitalism-exploit-2091718/. (Kathy G Mills collection)

86565184R00126

Made in the USA
Columbia, SC
08 January 2018